Business Diagnostics
2nd Edition

Richard Mimick

Michael Thompson

Note for Librarians: A cataloguing record for this book is available from
Library and Archives Canada at www.collectionscanada.ca/amicus/index-e.html
ISBN 1-55212-764-8

Design, typesetting and cover: R. Diment VRG

Printed in Victoria, BC, Canada. Printed on paper with minimum 30% recycled fibre.
Trafford's print shop runs on "green energy" from solar, wind and other environmentally-friendly power sources.

Offices in Canada, USA, Ireland and UK

Book sales for North America and international:
Trafford Publishing, 6E–2333 Government St.,
Victoria, BC V8T 4P4 CANADA
phone 250 383 6864 (toll-free 1 888 232 4444)
fax 250 383 6804; email to orders@trafford.com
Book sales in Europe:
Trafford Publishing (UK) Limited, 9 Park End Street, 2nd Floor
Oxford, UK OX1 1HH UNITED KINGDOM
phone 44 (0)1865 722 113 (local rate 0845 230 9601)
facsimile 44 (0)1865 722 868; info.uk@trafford.com
Order online at:
trafford.com/01-0164

10 9 8 7

TRAFFORD PUBLISHING™

Advance praise for 'Business Diagnostics'

A thorough but readable checklist approach to assessing (and managing) issues and opportunities that may impact your small business. Especially helpful in providing insights with respect to financing strategies from a commercial banker's perspective.

Donna Bridgeman
Vice President, Growthworks Capital
Working Opportunity Fund, Vancouver B.C

A recommended read – business is a dynamic and complex world, where time or limited skill sets can become impediments to good decision making.

Business practitioners at all levels will appreciate this practical book, full of proven strategies and diagnostic tools that can be quickly learned and immediately applied.

Francis Hartman MBA
National Director of Human Resources
Sleeman Breweries Limited

Business Diagnostics *is an innovative approach to one-stop business evaluation, development and growth. It is a welcome addition and should be included in any entrepreneurs' tool kit. The technology assessment chapter, in particular, is succinct and highly relevant to technology-based companies.*

Tim Walzak, President and CEO
Innovation and Development Corporation, University of Victoria, B.C

A major challenge to most business managers, especially those operating in the fast-paced world of high technology, is to find the time to learn good management practices while on the job; most people simply do not have the luxury of taking time off for formal training. Business Diagnostics *addresses this critical need by packaging the essentials into a manageable text.*

Denzil Doyle
Chairman, Capital Alliance Ventures Inc, Ottawa
Author – *Making Technology Happen*

The Business Diagnostics *text provides practical solutions for business professionals and effectively transforms theoretical concepts into real world insight....*

Andy Fraser MBA
Group Vice-President
FINNING (Canada)

If you are the CEO of a small to medium-sized company and want a pragmatic framework for sizing-up the health of your business, then I suggest you look at Rich and Mike's gem of a book, Business Diagnostics. *Track with the case study, use their novel size-up grids and you will have the pulse on your corporate health and a sound framework for revitalizing your business.*

T. John Drew
Chair, TEC (The Executive Committee), Victoria, B.C

I found your book one of the clearest guides to assessing a business that I came across in my 19 years with IRAP. Thank you for the efforts you made.

Alan M. Toon. P. Eng.
Industrial Technology Advisor. National Research Council – IRAP

Business Diagnostics *is a unique and highly valuable resource for technology companies. It is most readable in its style and covers the critical aspects of successfully leading, managing and growing a dynamic firm. Mimick and Thompson's perspective has answered a challenge by providing a 'required reading' for all technology firms, in fact, for all companies. Exceptionally well done.*

Doug Taylor, Former CEO
Vancouver Island Advanced Technology
VIATeC

Mike and Richard's book Business Diagnostics *provides sound and practical advice on 'sizing-up' any business. Regardless if you are a University learner or a seasoned business professional, readers will gain comprehensive business advice in a clear and concise format. That's not an easy task for any author, however Mike and Richard have made the process appear easy.*

Doug Galloway MBA
Regional Human Resources Manager, Home Depot Canada Inc.

ABOUT
THE AUTHORS

Rich Mimick is President and CEO of Professional Practice Management Services Limited, a management consulting and executive development firm based in Victoria. B.C. Rich holds a CPA (USA) designation and commenced his consulting career with Andersen Consulting.

His academic appointments include Chair and Professor at the world ranked Ivey Business School, Director of Royal Roads University Business Programs, and Director of University of Victoria's Executive Programs.

He is currently Director, Business, Management and Technology programs, Division of Continuing Studies, University of Victoria.

Rich has designed, developed and delivered consulting engagements and executive programs for Canadian, American, European and Asian clients. His areas of expertise are strategic management, finance and marketing strategy.

He has received international recognition for his outstanding teaching abilities and is known for his exceptional ability to turn complex topics into understandable practical learning.

Rich also provides consulting assistance in strategy and finance to various companies. He is a director and advisory board member of growth oriented companies and a past director of VIATeC, the Vancouver Island Advanced Technology Centre.

Mike Thompson has over 20 year's commercial banking experience gained in the U.K, Ontario and British Columbia, Canada.

He is presently Professor, Management Consulting at the Faculty of Management, Royal Roads University, Victoria, B.C.

Before commencing his academic career, Mike held a senior management positions at TD Commercial Banking and Bank of Montreal located in Victoria, British Columbia.

His academic credentials include an Honors degree in Economics from the University of Manchester and a Diploma in Land Economics from the University of British Columbia.

Professional certifications include Fellow of Institute of Canadian Bankers (FICB) and Certified Management Consultant (CMC).

Mike has taught Business Strategy courses at both the University of Victoria and Royal Roads University and has developed a number of successful business planning and risk assessment seminars for business and professional associations.

He is actively involved in the Victoria technology community, is a former director of the Vancouver Island Advanced Technology Centre (VIATeC) and is currently a board member of the Innovation and Development Corporation (IDC) at the University of Victoria.

CONTENTS

SECTION 1 THE EXTERNAL 'SIZE-UP'
Chapter 1 The Business Environment 3
Chapter 2 Industry Conditions 15

SECTION 2 THE INTERNAL 'SIZE-UP' 25
Chapter 3 The Financial Evaluation 27
Chapter 4 Marketing Strategy 51
Chapter 5 The Operations Review 65
Chapter 6 Human Resources Management 83
Chapter 7 The Technology Assessment 95

SECTION 3 THE COMPANY LIFE CYCLE AND RELATED FUNDING INITIATIVES
Chapter 8 New Business Opportunities and Strategies 111
Chapter 9 Sources of Equity Funding 129
Chapter 10 Managing Growth 143
Chapter 11 Sources of Debt Financing 157
Chapter 12 Survival Strategies 179

SECTION 4 STRATEGIC PLANNING
Chapter 13 The Business Planning Process 191

SECTION 5 CASE STUDY
Marston Control Devices Ltd. 209

APPENDIX 1 EXTERNAL AND INTERNAL 'SIZE-UP'
Marston Control Devices Ltd. 233

APPENDIX 2 CURRENT COMPANY VALUATION
Marston Control Devices Ltd. 247

APPENDIX 3 ENTERPRISE REVIEW SUMMARY
Marston Control Devices Ltd. 251

APPENDIX 4 PRELIMINARY ESTIMATE OF FUTURE VALUE FROM
AN INVESTOR'S PERSPECTIVE
Marston Control Devices Ltd. 257

REFERENCES AND RECOMMENDED READINGS 261

Preface and Acknowledgments

The origin of the Business Diagnostics concept can be traced to an early evening libation at Spinnakers Brew Pub, Victoria, B.C. in April 1995. We were both teaching a 'fast track' business strategy course for the University of Victoria and had been discussing the need to quickly and simply summarize business concepts for not only adult learners, but also business owners as well.

We decided to design a short, but informative business case and then perform a 'size up' on the subject company, assessing the relative attractiveness of the external environment and internal resources. This discussion led to the development of a successful one-day seminar series, which was anchored by a companion manual – "Size-Up Your Business".

Seminar participants provided us with positive feed back and encouragement to proceed to the next stage – the development of a more formal reference guide based upon the original size up model. Additional information was provided relating to the business life cycle and the challenges in raising debt and equity.

The research and writing of the Business Diagnostics book took place between April 2000 and February 2001. We received tremendous support and encouragement from the Victoria business and technology community and would like to acknowledge the specific contributions of the following people:

Nicole Burgess helped create the layout of the earlier generation Size-Up guide.

Chris Green provided some helpful early stage external environment research while John and David Thompson assisted with preliminary development of selected diagrams and word processing support.

Joe Misius provided invaluable editorial review and feedback. Chris Tilbe completed some outstanding work in assisting with the time intensive early stage document word processing.

The manuscript review process was greatly simplified by helpful feedback from the following people:

Pat Trelawny, Arthur Roberts, Q.C., Ken Glover, C.A., Gerry McQuade, Andrew Jackson C.A., Trevor Orme, Tim McColl, Mike Marley, Brian Dyer, C.A., Darin and Bonnie Reeves, Dawn Wattie, Keith Reed, Vern Fischer, Bob Hunter, Roger Palmer, Craig Thomson, Tony Melli, Frank Bourree, Charles Layton and Bob Williamson.

Bill Cooke and Colin Lennox from the Vancouver Island Advanced Technology Centre (VIATeC) along with John Simmons provided invaluable feedback, especially on the equity funding process. Vern Fitzgerald, C.A made a significant contribution to the initial Size-Up seminar through the provision of current tax strategies for business owners.

Roy Diment (Vivencia Resources Group) completed the book graphic design and layout while Bruce Batchelor, CEO, Trafford Publishing, provided wise counsel and support through the publishing process. Deborah Wright of Precision Proofreading edited the draft edition with an eagle eye for detail.

Ron Lou-Poy, Q.C. attended to legal documentation issues relating to the publication, while Ian Ferguson and Mike Kynaston of the West Coast Group provided helpful strategic insights as to the future generation of Business Diagnostic guides.

In Fall 2005, we decided to commence the *Business Diagnostics 2nd Edition* which contains updates to various chapters, along with an expanded set of Size-Up grids which will allow a more detailed evaluation of the Marston Control Devices case.

The updating process was greatly assisted with the help of the following people:

Dr. Susan Halfhill (Industry Conditions), Allen Colpitts (Financial Evaluation), Marnie Anderson and Lois Fearon (Marketing Strategy), Jonathan Andrews (Technology Assessment) and Bill Cooke (Sources of Equity Funding).

Roy Diment (VRG) has again provided wonderful support with the book graphic design and layout, while Betina Albornoz developed some excellent diagrams.

Last but certainly not least, special thanks and acknowledgment is given to our respective spouses, Claudia and Kathy, for their continued patience and cheerful encouragement.

Richard Mimick and Michael Thompson

Victoria, B.C.
January 2007

INTRODUCTION

Business Diagnostics has been written to overcome a significant challenge facing today's business owners, specifically the time constraints in acquiring business management skills.

Business owners have limited time or inclination to attend extended business school courses. Likewise, accessing topical information on enhancing corporate performance (magazines or web sites) can be sporadic and time consuming.

The authors have designed *Business Diagnostics* to address these concerns by developing a valuable reference book that can be easily read over a weekend or a few weekday evenings.

Business Diagnostics will provide practical assistance to the following target audiences:

> ➤ The existing business owner or manager who has growth opportunities and needs to 'size up' existing and potential operations.

> ➤ The individual planning to buy or invest in another business. That process requires the completion of 'diagnostic checks' to ensure that the targeted entity has the required degree of corporate health.

> ➤ The individual who wishes to set up a new, yet to be proven, business venture and requires guidelines to assess the likelihood of success and the steps necessary to attract financing or equity.

> ➤ A new or existing technology company owner who needs to assess the relative merits of attracting outside equity capital or raising additional debt in order to expand product lines and/or markets.

We also feel that this book will be useful to Business students by providing a concise set of practical diagnostic tools to complement generic course materials. At the same time, the material will provide a fast track to understanding the fundamentals and challenges in running and growing a company.

Readers will gain practical insights into the following key areas:

Sections 1 and 2: Instructs the reader how to size-up a business operation, assessing its relative strengths and weaknesses.

The *External size-up* examines the business environment (political, economic, societal and technological factors) along with prevailing industry conditions.

The *Internal size-up* then drills down into the individual company's performance, evaluating its relative health from different viewpoints – Financial, Marketing, Operations, Human Resources, and Technology.

Section 3: Explains company life cycles and how the various sources of funding (equity and debt) can be accessed. Survival and turnaround strategies are also evaluated. Recognizing potential danger signals is increasingly important given today's rapidly changing business environment.

Section 4: Provides tips and insights on the effective completion of Strategic Business plans.

Section 5: Consists of a short case study of a fictitious company (Marston Control Devices). Readers utilize the size up techniques covered in earlier sections to assess the company's health and prospects by completing optional size-up work sheets as part of the evaluation process.

Marston Control Devices Ltd. is also seeking investment capital and readers have the opportunity to expand their size-up skills by completing a preliminary company valuation and reviewing the capital raising process by way of a tactical Enterprise Review Summary.

These five sections are inter-related and are summarized in the diagram opposite.

Appendices: Provide the author's suggested size-up summaries, company valuations and sample Enterprise Review Summary to round out the learning process.

The 2nd edition of *Business Diagnostics* contains some updated materials and insights based upon the authors' teaching and consulting experiences over the past four years since the original edition was published.

Business Diagnostics Overview

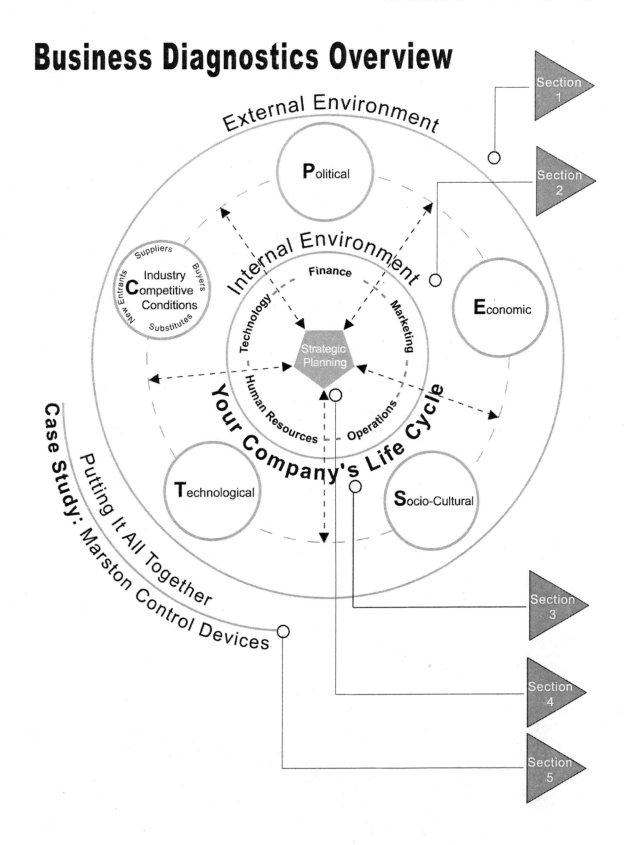

SECTION 1

THE EXTERNAL 'SIZE-UP'

Business Diagnostics Overview

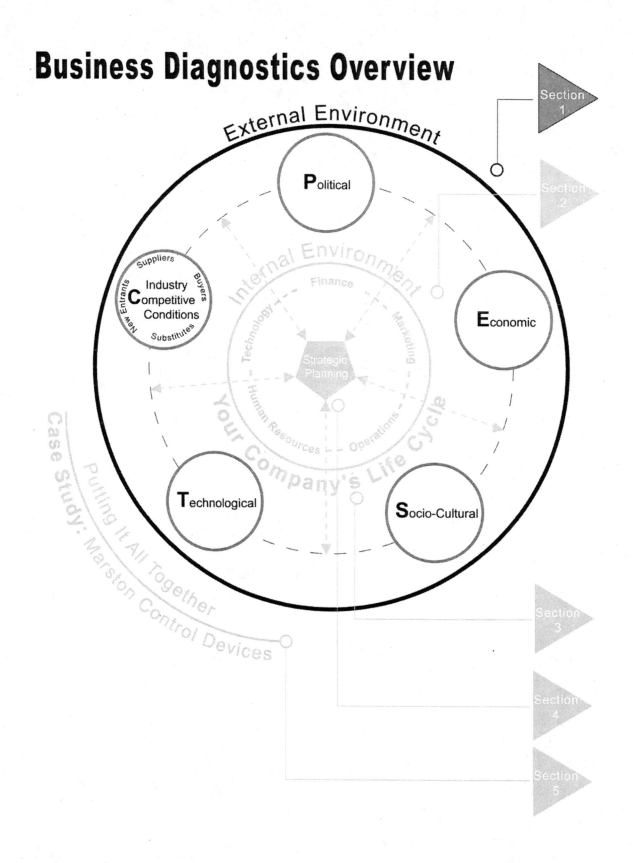

CHAPTER 1
THE BUSINESS ENVIRONMENT

OVERVIEW

A key element of the External Size-Up process is looking at 'the Big Picture'. The prevailing business environment and related industry conditions need to be critically reviewed by company management.

This chapter covers the Business Environment. Think of it as an outer atmosphere that, while distinct from day to day company operations, exerts a significant impact on the company's prospects and performance.

A useful tool to assess the Business Environment is a P.E.S.T. analysis, an easy-to-remember acronym that encompasses the following four key areas:

- Political Factors
- Economic Issues
- Socio – Cultural Trends
- Technological Considerations

Each key area is reviewed, providing a checklist of issues to consider. While some of these issues are industry specific (i.e. they relate to the industry within which a company operates or plans to operate), the focus of this chapter remains the big picture.

The P.E.S.T. structure and the impact on an individual company is illustrated in Figure 1-1 below.

Figure 1-1

P.E.S.T. – An Overview

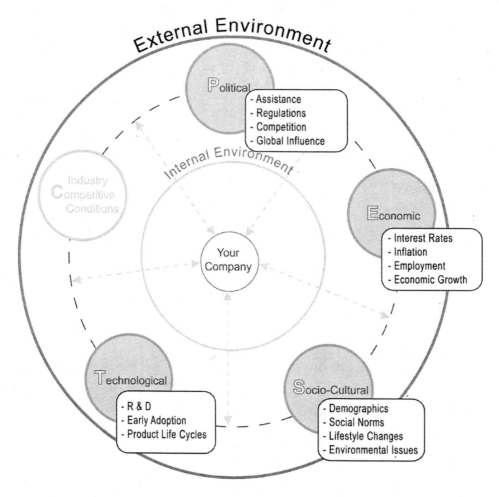

POLITICAL FACTORS

The predominant force here is government influence, ranging from global entities to federal to provincial to municipal or a combination of all four.

You should be aware that governments could:

➤ Assist you

➤ Regulate you

➤ Compete with you

➤ Globally influence you

Consider your company and the industry in which it operates and then review the following checklist to determine the extent to which government activities influence your business environment. It is also worthwhile to assess the extent of business friendly policies implemented by your provincial, federal, and governments.

> ➤ Is new legislation pending that may change their approach?

> ➤ Will the political climate change in the near term? What impact will this have on your business?

We have also added an additional section – Global Influences, which recognizes the dramatic influence that 'trans-national' events, markets and organizations now exert.

GOVERNMENT ASSISTANCE TO BUSINESS

Is government support available for:

> ➤ Industrial research?

> ➤ Technological innovation?

> ➤ Export opportunities?

> ➤ Financing?

> ➤ Employment programs?

Remember:

If grants or subsidies are available, are they also available to your competitors? Are there any strings attached?

LEGAL REGULATION OF BUSINESS

How do the following regulatory mechanisms impact your business:

> ➤ Taxation: Will reduce your return on investment and may increase or decrease your competitive advantage if your company faces lower or higher tax-rates than your competition?

> ➤ Health and safety regulations?

> ➤ Environmental policies and controls: Incentives, fees, penalties, and potential project delays?

➤ Regulating competition: An example is the Federal Competition Act, which prohibits certain practices, like tied selling, exclusive dealing, discriminatory allowances, etc.

➤ Consumer protection: Examples would include the Food and Drug Act and the Hazardous Products Act.

➤ Investor protection: Various Securities Acts

➤ Protection of firms' intangible assets: Trademarks, patents, copyrights, and industrial design.

➤ Post Enron: Sarbanes –Oxley (USA) and C.S.A (Canadian Securities Administrators) governance compliance requirements.

DIRECT COMPETITION WITH BUSINESS

➤ Crown corporations (government owned) can be unpredictable competitors with deep pockets.

➤ Privatization of government agencies can intensify competitive pressures by altering traditional buying and selling practices.

GLOBAL INFLUENCES

➤ Significant political events like 9/11, Berlin Wall removal

➤ Emerging new global markets and competitors in China, India and Russia

➤ Transnational bureaucracies like WTO, Geneva and the European Union H.Q. in Brussels.

To round out this review of the external political factors, we would recommend reading *The World Is Flat: A Brief History of the 21st Century* by Thomas Friedman. This book sets out to explain how the 'flattening' of the world business 'playing field' has evolved through a convergence of technology and the explosion of the middle-class in China and India.

Friedman describes 10 'flatteners' – major political events, innovations and companies that have converged to deliver multiple new tools and processes for collaboration on a global scale.[1]

ECONOMIC ISSUES

The state of the economy has an obvious impact on your business yet many business owners are confused by the overwhelming weight of economic data and information available to them. There are over one hundred economic indicators published on a regular basis by financial and economic analysts and government agencies. This section separates the trees from the forest by summarizing the six key areas of macro economic activity that will impact the business owner.

KEY MACRO ECONOMIC INDICATORS

1. Economic Growth

2. Price levels (inflation)

3. Interest rates

4. Employment

5. Government policy

6. Global economic influences, notably resource price shocks

1. ECONOMIC GROWTH

- The primary indicator is Gross Domestic Product (GDP), which measures a country's economic output.

- Recent GDP growth rates of 3-4% in North America have indicated robust, growing economies accompanied by strong consumer confidence and spending.

- Real GDP recognizes that the effect of inflation on price levels has been removed, thereby providing a more accurate fix on actual economic growth.

- Three consecutive (three month) quarters of decline in GDP growth are generally considered to indicate the onset of a recession.

2. PRICE LEVELS

- The prevailing level of price inflation has a crucial effect on consumer confidence along with business revenue and earnings performance.

➤ The primary indicator is the Consumer Price Index (CPI) that is the traditional yardstick for tracking inflation.

➤ The CPI measures the relative price increases of a 'basket' of goods and services. (The index's accuracy has been questioned in the past for its susceptibility to interest rate swings, short-term erratic price fluctuations and the extent to which energy and food costs have been included).

➤ Inflation can be broadly segmented as follows:

    i) *Demand Pull*: Prices are 'pulled' up by strong consumer and business demand for goods and services.

    ii) *Cost Push*: Prices are 'pushed' up by increased raw material and labour costs.

3. INTEREST RATES

➤ They are a key influence on economic activity. Both short- and long-term rates need to be considered.

➤ Short-term rates (one to twelve months) are set by the Bank of Canada and/or the U.S Federal Reserve Bank and exert a significant impact on consumer credit and business borrowings.

➤ Long-term rates (one to twenty years) follow corporate and government bond markets. These rates have a major impact on consumer big-ticket purchases and business expansion/capital expenditure decisions.

➤ The relationship between short-term and long-term interest rates has historically been defined by a positive yield curve with short-term rates lower than long-term rates (investors require a greater reward to lock in investments for a longer time period).

➤ An inverted yield curve (short-term rates higher than long-term rates) is often considered to be a precursor to a recession.

Figure 1-2 (opposite) provides a graphical representation of positive and negative yield curves.

Figure 1-2

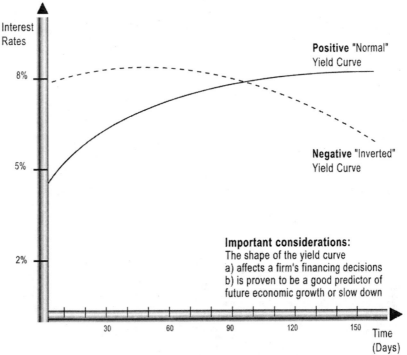

Yield Curves

> Interest rates may have a significant impact on a company's financial performance and strategies. For example, in a rising interest rate environment, the company's ability to repay debt will be impaired (higher interest costs, less principal paid back).

> Even if an early stage company has been funded by equity (as opposed to debt financing), increasing interest rates will tend to exert a dampening effect on overall economic growth prospects.

4. EMPLOYMENT

> The primary indicator of labor market health is the percentage of the available workforce that is unemployed. Rates close to the 3-4% level indicate 'full employment'.

> There are significant differences in the kinds of employment experienced by workers and the resulting impact on the economy. Some are:

    i) *Frictional unemployment:* Workers temporarily out of work.

    ii) *Cyclical unemployment:* Workers without jobs due to downturns in business cycles (i.e. shipbuilding, auto sector).

    iii) *Structural unemployment:* People out of work for long periods of time due to lack of skills (e.g. pursuing higher education) or fundamental changes in economic resources (e.g., East Coast fishery).

5. GOVERNMENT ACTIVITIES AND POLICIES

Consider:

- ➤ The current levels of direct and indirect taxes compared to competitors' countries.

- ➤ The potential for transfer payment cutbacks (federal to provincial to local governments).

- ➤ The level of government spending, which is impacted by current fiscal budget performance.

- ➤ More recently, the USA running massive trade and budget deficits, is starting to cause considerable concern as increasing (downward) pressure is applied to the US dollar

6. GLOBAL ECONOMIC INFLUENCES

Key areas to assess:

- ➤ Currency value: The relative value of the Canadian versus the US dollar has a major impact on exporters and importers. While short-term fluctuations are difficult to anticipate, longer-term trends can often be identified and hedged against by forward exchange rate contracts available through your bank.

- ➤ Trading arrangements: Free trade areas versus economies that remain protected by tariffs and quotas. Examples include NAFTA, and the EC.

- ➤ Global markets: The rise of monopolistic multinationals with enormous buying power and economies of scale.

- ➤ Preferential treatment: Countries imposing 'buy at home' policies on government departments and agencies to ensure local companies have 'first-to-market' opportunities.

SOCIO-CULTURAL TRENDS

While societal and cultural trends take time to unfold, the sheer force and momentum of them may have significant implications for business owners.

Consider the following:

- ➤ *Global population trends:* The current world population is 6 billion + with China/India accounting for approx. 2.5 billion and experiencing unprecedented economic growth.

➤ *Demographics:* The baby boomer generation in North America, born between 1948 and 1962 are now starting to enter their retirement years. How will it affect your marketplace?

➤ *Psychographics:* Behavioral, lifestyle and psychological factors that impact purchasing patterns (i.e. environmental concerns and 'green products').

➤ *Ethnic distribution:* In the USA, significant increases in a Hispanic and Asian work-forces are forecast, especially on the West Coast

➤ *Social changes:*

- ◆ The blended family. Divorced couples remarrying and blending each other's children into a new family unit.
- ◆ The rise of consumerism. The needs of consumers (perceived and real) and the importance in serving them with integrity and honesty.
- ◆ Dual income families, no children.

➤ *Lifestyle changes:*

- ◆ Telecommuting and 'hoffices' (home based offices)
- ◆ Early/post retirement issues.
- ◆ Dual career couples
- ◆ Retraining as boomers commence second careers.
- ◆ Employee mobility to competitors

➤ *Work force diversity requirements*

➤ *Women-owned* small and medium-sized businesses

➤ *Contract employees* arising from past corporate restructurings

➤ *Environmental awareness:*

- ◆ Health and safety issues (Aging population and related health care issues)
- ◆ International agreements like the Kyoto Protocol
- ◆ "Green" products.
- ◆ Recycling and conservation issues.
- ◆ Environmental waste clean up.

Technological Considerations

It is crucial to follow current technology trends both outside and within your industry segments.

Consider Moore's law which states that while prices keep constant, the processing power of microchips doubles every 18 months.

Early adopters of new technologies often derive greater market share and improved returns on their capital investment.

Technology issues to review:

➤ The Internet as a source of data and information – how is your company exploiting these opportunities?

➤ The advent of wireless handheld devices leading to substantial increases in 'business connectivity' – does this include you?

➤ What are the Research and Development (R&D) requirements for your industry segment? How do your company's **actual** R&D expenditures compare? Are you falling behind?

➤ The continued importance of Business-to-Business (B2B) e-commerce. Is your company an electronic buyer or seller or both? How does this impact existing client and supplier relationships?

➤ How will current technology changes impact your company's operations:

- Product life cycles (likely shorter and shorter).
- Competitors who are more technology savvy.
- Ability to forge corporate alliances or joint ventures.
- Access to international markets.
- Delivery (just in time) and transportation issues.
- Potential for process improvements and cost savings.
- Ability to meet customer needs.

USEFUL WEB SITES

www.statcan.ca	StatsCanada – latest economic indicators
www.eurunion.com	European Union
www.nafta.com	NAFTA
www.usitc.gov	U.S. International Trade Commission
www.easidemographics.com	Demographic data for target markets
www.rdmag.com	Online resources for R&D professionals
www.brint.com	eBusiness information portal
www.guardian.co.uk	In depth coverage global PEST issues
www.outsourcing.com	The Outsourcing Institute

Notes from text.

1. Thomas Friedman, *The World is Flat: A brief History of the 21st Century.*

Notes

CHAPTER 2
INDUSTRY CONDITIONS

OVERVIEW

The next stage in reviewing the External Business environment is to conduct an in-depth assessment of the industry segment in which your company operates. Industry prospects and risks have a fundamental impact on a firm's performance and strategy.

The following section provides a high-level industry evaluation followed by a more localized assessment of industry competitive conditions. We also address the importance of defining your competitive advantages and also determining how you measure up to other competitors in your industry segment.

Rounding out this process will be a review of the industry assessment models detailed in the recently published book, Blue Ocean Strategy by W. Chan Kim and Renee Mauborgne.

1. INDUSTRY EVALUATION

This evaluation involves an examination of the characteristics and trends resident in your industry sector. The following assessment process is suggested:

➤ Complete an industry description: This is a concise summary that identifies the industry's market size and growth. Other factors to consider will include: geographic scope, number of competitors, pace of technological change, innovation, and the number and size of buyers and sellers.

➤ Assess typical capital requirements. Is the industry fixed asset or working capital intensive? Or both?

➤ Determine the industry vulnerability to PEST factors (covered in Chapter One):

- ◆ Macro economic conditions?
- ◆ Political, legal or regulatory issues?
- ◆ Environmental concerns and /technological trends?
- ◆ Demographic influences?

➤ Consider the life-cycle stage of the industry segment.

By examining the product, service, and market life-cycle stages, you can pinpoint the present age of your industry segment as follows:

Age Categories

- ◆ Early stage?
- ◆ Growth?
- ◆ Shake-out?
- ◆ Maturity?
- ◆ Decline?

➤ Conduct an industry 'business system' analysis.
This involves the identification of supply and distribution channels used in the industry segment and assessing which are the most efficient.

➤ Assess Driving Forces. These are factors that may exert major future change in your industry segment.

Examples of Driving Forces include:

➤ Globalization of industry segments (remember our reference to *The World Is Flat* in Chapter 1).

➤ The Internet and related e-commerce opportunities or threats.

➤ Significant change in buyer's tastes and needs.

➤ New methods of marketing or distributing products.

➤ Entry or exit of major firms.

➤ Fundamental changes in government regulatory policies or societal attitudes.

➤ New technologies that open up new values and benefits (i.e. increased bandwidth from fiber optic transmissions).

These driving forces should be assessed to determine either a positive (+) or negative (-) influence.

2. INDUSTRY COMPETITIVE CONDITIONS

Having completed the industry evaluation, the next step is to assess the competitive environment.

A key question to ask: Is this an industry that we want to operate within, given the relative intensity of competition?

An effective way to assess competitive forces within an industry segment is to use Michael Porter's *Five Forces* model.[1] The model provides a framework that allows the analysis of the primary competitive forces prevalent within an industry segment.

Figure 2-1 (next page) illustrates the relationship between various companies operating within a specific industry segment which, in turn, is impacted by various competitive forces.

The Five Forces are detailed below along with some reflective questions that allow you to gauge the relative intensity of the forces.

THREAT OF NEW ENTRANTS OR BARRIERS TO ENTRY

- ➤ Are there high dollar levels of capital required to enter?
- ➤ Do existing players have the ability to retaliate via pricing or new product strategies?
- ➤ Is it difficult to obtain the necessary skilled personnel or materials?
- ➤ Is it difficult to get regulatory approvals?

BARGAINING POWER OF CUSTOMERS (BUYER POWER)

- ➤ Will customers face significant switching costs to other sellers?
- ➤ Do your customers recognize your product as unique?
- ➤ Are there multiple other sellers available to customers?

BARGAINING POWER OF SUPPLIERS (SUPPLIER POWER)

- ➤ Are there other potential suppliers?
- ➤ Do purchases and direct labor (cost of goods sold – COGS) have a significant impact on overall costs?

Figure 2-1

Industry Competitive Assessment

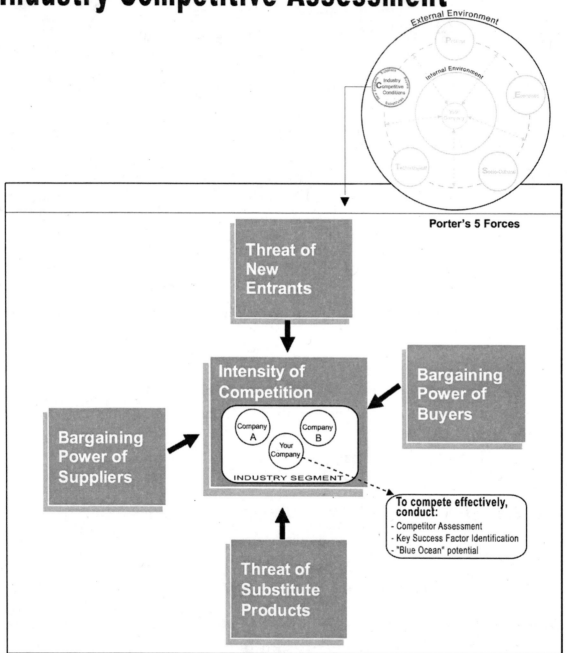

THREAT OF SUBSTITUTE PRODUCTS

➤ Are customers unlikely or unable to switch to substitute products offered by firms in other industries or different types of products?

➤ Will customers incur costs when switching to substitutes?

INTENSITY OF RIVALRY AMONG EXISTING COMPETITORS

➤ Is the industry segment growing rapidly-thereby accommodating new competitors?

➤ Is competition local, national, or global?

To assess the level of competition in your industry segment, the forces can be ranked on the following table:

EVALUATION OF INDUSTRY COMPETITIVE CONDITIONS

	Favorable	Neutral	Unfavorable
Threat of New Entrants	Low	Medium	High
Bargaining Power of Customers	Low	Medium	High
Bargaining Power of Suppliers	Low	Medium	High
Threat of Substitutes	Low	Medium	High
Intensity of Rivalry between Competitors	Low	Medium	High

By asking and answering the five sector questions and using the table, you can determine if the relevant force is favorable, neutral, or unfavorable to the overall competitive environment.

After understanding these competitive forces individually, it is useful to consider the impact of all five forces of competition collectively. In general, the stronger *the collective impact* of the five competitive forces, the harder it is for rival companies in this industry to be profitable.

A classic example is the restaurant industry where the five forces are generally 'unfavourable' and many operators struggle to maintain a profitable performance.

A note on using the Evaluation Grids:

You determine that Threat of New Entrants is **Low.** This would be considered a **favorable** influence allowing your firm to survive and prosper in its particular Industry segment.

Likewise, you determine that Bargaining Power of Suppliers is **High**. This would be considered an **unfavorable** influence and should lead you to consider strategies to overcome their influence. One solution might be to reduce supplier concentration by adopting a B2B purchasing model that could open up new sources of supply.

The key point here is that the more your company's strategy insulates you from competitive pressures, the more effective it will be.

3. COMPETITOR ASSESSMENT

After reviewing your industry's competitive environment, the next step is to complete an assessment of the identified competition.

A useful process is to determine what factors or influences have contributed to the competitive strength of your industry peers.

Consider the following:

- ➤ Economies of scale?
- ➤ Internal functional capabilities?
- ➤ Deep pockets (sufficient financial resources to meet working capital requirements and deter new entrants)?
- ➤ Government regulatory protection afforded to them?
- ➤ Superior distribution channels?
- ➤ Brand image that differentiates them?
- ➤ Their future strategic objectives?

To gain an accurate fix on competition and industry segment trends, consider the following useful intelligence sources:

- ➤ *Your Employees.* They will likely have current knowledge about your competition and how they measure up in your industry segment. Ask them!

- ➤ *Industry Associations and Directories* (Dun & Bradstreet, local Chamber of Commerce, etc.)

- ➤ *Your Customers.* Ask them how you measure up against your competitors.

- ➤ *Commercial Databases* (Dow Jones, InfoGlobe).

- ➤ *Internet.* Competitors' web sites and online media archives.

- ➤ *Strategis* (Industry Canada web page).

- ➤ *Securities firm's research reports.* Select those firms where analysts are top ranked for a particular industry sector.

4. COMPETITIVE ADVANTAGE

To grow and prosper in your industry segment, it is crucial to create and maintain a strong sustainable competitive advantage over your competitors. One of the best ways to accomplish this to identify your industry's Key Success Factors (KSFs) and then be distinctively better than competitors on one or two of the KSFs.

Key success factors (KSFs) are special skills and resources that must be possessed to gain a competitive advantage in a particular industry segment. All firms in the particular industry sector must pay close attention to them – KSFs are competitive factors that determine whether industry participants will be financially and strategically successful.

Some examples:

- ◆ Cost advantages
- ◆ Quality advantages
- ◆ Unique technology allied with intellectual property protection
- ◆ Specialized manufacturing process
- ◆ Location (proximity to materials, skilled employees, and markets)
- ◆ Effective and efficient distribution channels
- ◆ Highly skilled workforce
- ◆ Ability to navigate regulatory approval processes
- ◆ Favorable image and reputation with clients

For example, the Wine industry has the following desired KSFs:

> ➤ Full utilization of winemaking capacity

> ➤ A comprehensive network of wholesale distributors and re-sellers.

> ➤ Creative promotion tactics – to differentiate in an overcrowded market-place

Thus to compete successfully in the wine industry, a company must possess all three of these KSFs, but to have **competitive advantage** it must execute these KSFs distinctively better than competitors.

5) POTENTIAL FOR A 'BLUE OCEAN STRATEGY'

This final section is based upon a recently published book titled 'Blue Ocean Strategy: How to Create Uncontested Market Space and Make the Competition Irrelevant', authored by W. Chan Kim and Renée Mauborgne.

The central message is that tomorrow's leading companies will succeed not by battling competitors but by creating 'blue oceans' of uncontested market space, ripe for growth. This is in dramatic contrast to many of today's overcrowded industries where heads on competition results in nothing more that a 'bloody red ocean' of rivals fighting over a shrinking profit pool.

The Blue Ocean Strategy consists of six principles:

1) Reconstruct market boundaries – in order to break from the competition and the accepted boundaries that define how they compete.

2) Focus on the big picture -the need to move from a smorgasbord of tactics to the preparation of a strategy canvas which unlocks the creativity of people within the organization.

The strategy canvas consists of a horizontal and vertical axis.

The horizontal axis captures the range of factors that an industry competes on and invests in. For example, within the U. S. wine industry, the canvas would map factors like price per bottle of wine, the need for a refined packaging image, the aging quality wine and the prestige of the wine vinyard.

The vertical axis captures the offering level (low to high) that buyers receive across the competing factors that are detailed on the horizontal axis.

3) Reach beyond existing demand – instead of concentrating on existing customers, you need to look to non-customers. Example: Callaway Golf who aggregated new demand for its big Bertha club by looking to non-customers who were looking for a large club head to lessen the difficulty of their golf game.

4) Get the Strategic Sequence right – following a four step process:

- ♦ Is there exceptional buyer utility in your business idea?
- ♦ Is your price easily accessible to the majority of buyers?
- ♦ Can you attain your cost targets?
- ♦ What are the adoption hurdles in implementing your business idea?

5) Overcome Organizational Hurdles – the need to win employees backing in order to break from the status quo

6) Build Execution into Strategy – to minimize the management risk of distrust and non cooperation

The *litmus test* for an effective Blue Ocean Strategy is captured by these three following characteristics:

Is there *Focus* – Southwest Airlines emphasizes only three factors – friendly service, speed and frequent point-to-point departures.

Is there *Divergence* – Southwest pioneered point-to-point travel between midsize cities as opposed to the industry norm of operating through a hub and spoke system

Is there a *Compelling tagline* – [yellowtail wine] can be captured as 'a fun and simple wine to be enjoyed everyday'

USEFUL WEB SITES:

www.ceoexpress.com	CEO Express
www.cyberatlas.com	Statistics and web marketing information
www.bizminer.com	Industry reports
www.kpmg.ca	KPMG Industries – Specialized reports
www.bluebook.ca	Online database search engine – Canadian companies
www.sedar.com	Database information on Canadian public companies

Notes from text.

1. Michael Porter. *Competitive Strategy: Techniques for Analyzing Industries and Competitiors*. New York Free Press 1980.

NOTES

SECTION 2

THE INTERNAL 'SIZE-UP'

Business Diagnostics Overview

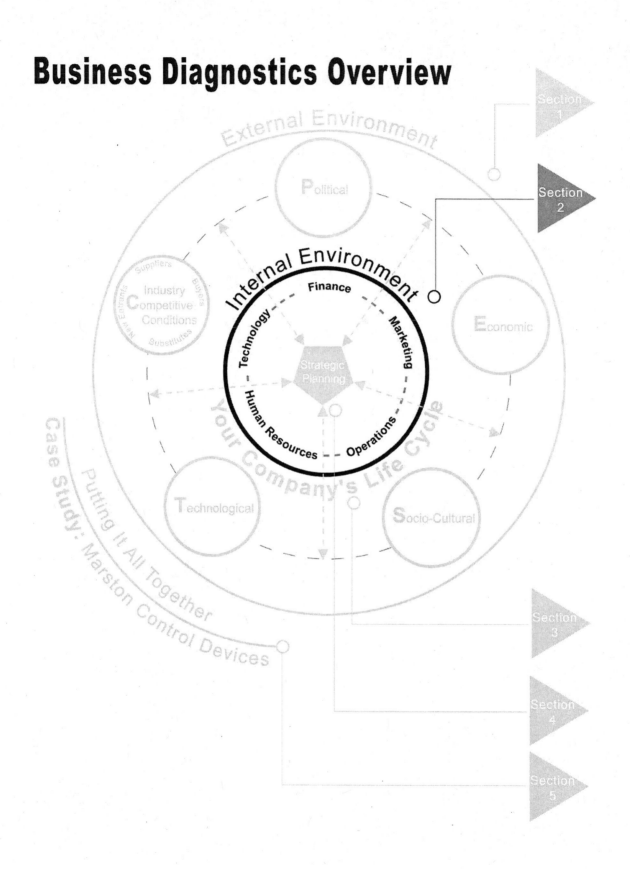

CHAPTER 3
THE FINANCIAL EVALUATION

OVERVIEW

This chapter deals with the financial health of your company – a crucial component to your survival and success. We will look at six key areas:

Financial Statements

This section provides an overview of the Balance Sheet, Income Statement, and Statement of Cash Flows, along with a brief summary of the types of financial statement presentations that are available.

Financial Goals and Ratio Analysis

The six key indicators of your corporate financial health are presented. We also demystify ratio analysis and show you how to build an effective diagnostic toolbox.

Financial Projections

An overview of pro forma Balance Sheet, Income, and Cash Flow Statements that forecast your anticipated financial performance in the future.

Managing 'Cash Drivers'

Some useful tips to manage your working capital and cash cycles are outlined.

Break-even Analysis

A concise explanation of the relationship between revenue and fixed/variable costs is provided.

Capital Budgeting Techniques

An overview of longer term investment decision making is presented.

FINANCIAL STATEMENTS

Financial statements are essential tools that are used to analyze and assess your business performance.

> ➢ Lenders require them to expedite loan applications.

> ➢ Company owners need them to track financial performance and to determine their financial health.

> ➢ Suppliers often want to review them in order to grant credit and to ensure that new clients can pay them.

> ➢ Clients may check them to reassure themselves that their key suppliers will be around for a while.

The following three separate, yet closely interrelated financial statements, will be reviewed:

1. The Balance Sheet: provides a snapshot of a company's financial position at a set point in time.

2. The Income (or profit and loss or operating) Statement: reveals the company's revenue, expenses, and profit performance over a specific period of time.

3. The Cash Flow Statement: indicates how much and by what means cash was generated by the company over a specific time and how it was used.

1. THE BALANCE SHEET

The Balance Sheet lists and totals the assets, liabilities, and owners' equity at the end of an operating period (i.e. December 31st, 2001). The relationship between assets and liabilities is shown by the following formula.

$$\text{ASSETS} - \text{LIABILITIES} = \text{OWNERS' EQUITY}$$

Assets: Consist of cash and items you can easily convert into cash (like securities and accounts receivable), and include items you need to make products and provide services (like inventory, equipment, or machinery). Assets on the Balance Sheet are usually listed in order of how quickly each can be converted into cash or liquidity.

Liabilities: Are amounts owed by the company and are usually classified as Current Liabilities (due within one year) or Long-term Liabilities which are listed according to how soon each liability has to be repaid.

Owners or Shareholders equity: Reflects the funds contributed to the company for ownership interest as well as the accumulation of profits or losses derived in the past (Retained Earnings).

An example of a Balance Sheet is shown below:

ABC Company						
Balance Sheet						
As of December 31, 2000						
(thousands of dollars)						
Assets			1999		2000	Change
Current Assets:						
Cash			$ 4,000		$ 1,800	-$ 2,200
Marketable securities			$ 2,000		$ 2,000	
Accounts receivable			$ 4,000		$ 5,000	$ 1,000
Inventory			$ 4,000		$ 4,600	$ 600
Prepaid expenses			$ 200		$ 200	
Total Current Assets			$ 14,200		$ 13,600	-$ 600
Property, Plant, And Equipment						
Historical cost	$ 10,000			$ 12,000		
Less accumulated depreciation	$ 6,000	$ 4,000		$ 6,400	$ 5,600	$ 1,600
Other Assets						
Investment in subsidiary		$ 800			$ 800	
Total Assets		$ 19,000			$ 20,000	$ 1,000
Liabilities & Owners' Equity						
Current Liabilities:						
Accounts payable		$ 600			$ 1,000	$ 400
Accrued expenses		$ 2,600			$ 2,400	-$ 200
Current portion of long-term debt		$ 400			$ 400	
Total Current Liabilities		$ 3,600			$ 3,800	$ 200
Long-term Debt		$ 4,000			$ 3,600	-$ 400
Total Liabilities		$ 7,600			$ 7,400	
Shareholders' Equity:						
Capital Stock	$ 4,000			$ 4,000		
Retained Earnings	$ 7,400	$ 11,400		$ 8,600	$ 12,600	$ 1,200
Total Liabilities & Shareholders Equity		$ 19,000			$ 20,000	$ 1,000

2. INCOME STATEMENT (PROFIT OR LOSS)

➤ Indicates how much money the company made or lost over a reporting period.

➤ The statement shows revenues generated from selling goods and/or services with the Cost of Goods Sold (COGS), operating expenses, financing costs, and taxes deducted to arrive at a net income figure.

The following statement summarizes the key components:

ABC Company Income Statement For the year ending December 31, 2000 (thousands of dollars)		
Net Sales		$ 20,000
Cost of goods sold		$ 14,000
Gross Profit		$ 6,000
Operating Expenses:		
Selling	$ 1,200	
Administrative	$ 2,000	
Depreciation	$ 400	$ 3,600
Income from operations		$ 2,400
Interest expense		$ 400
Income before taxes		$ 2,000
Income tax expense		$ 800
Net Income		$ 1,200

PROFIT, EARNINGS, AND INCOME

These terms are often interchanged and for the purposes of this chapter, essentially have the same meaning.

3. THE CASH FLOW STATEMENT
(STATEMENT OF CHANGES IN FINANCIAL POSITION)

Remember that revenue is not necessarily received when it is earned and expenses are not always paid when incurred, so it is important to chart the inflow or outflow of cash experienced by the company. The following statement shows the flows of cash (sources and uses) within a company for an operating period of one year. Make note of how the cash flows tie in with the changes to the Balance Sheet and to the Income Statement as outlined on the previous pages.

ABC Company		
Statement of Cash Flow		
For the year ending December 31, 2000		
(thousands of dollars)		
Cash flow from Operations:		
Net income	$	1,200
Depreciation (non cash item)	$	400
	$	1,600
Changes in:		
Accounts receivable	$	(1,000)
Inventory	$	(600)
Accounts payable	$	400
Accrued expenses	$	(200)
Net cash provided by Operations	$	200
Cash flows from investing activities:		
Purchase of capital assets	$	(2,000)
Net Cash from financing activities:		
Repayment of long-term debt		(400)
Net cash provided (used)	**$**	**(2,200)**

TYPES OF FINANCIAL STATEMENTS

While financial statements provide critical information to company owners, the *basis of presentation* and the *source* of the information deserve careful consideration.

a) Basis of presentation

Company owners need to ensure that their financial statements are prepared in accordance with Generally Accepted Accounting Principles (GAAP). This process ensures that the financial data is consistently presented, thereby allowing meaningful comparison between time periods.

A key principle called *full disclosure* compels management to ensure that all liabilities and material facts are presented.

b) The source and integrity of the information

In Canada, you will encounter three types of financial statements that provide different levels of comfort to their readers.

1) *Notice to Reader*

Essentially a compilation of the company owners' financial records with no verifications or limited investigation completed by the external accountant.

2) *Review Engagement:*

Greater comfort is provided by certain tests and verifications that are completed by the accountant and accompanied by detailed explanatory notes. The resulting financial statements are the most common form of presentation and are usually acceptable to most investors, bankers or suppliers.

3) *Audited Financial Statements:*

These are the most expensive and comprehensive and are normally completed by large private firms, public companies, and government institutions.

FINANCIAL GOALS AND RATIO ANALYSIS

OVERVIEW

To effectively assess a company's relative financial health, we present six key indicators that you should consider.

These key indicators are presented along with brief explanations. The financial ratios (diagnostic tests) which are pertinent to each category are also provided.

1. PROFITABILITY AND CASH FLOW

➤ Gross Profit

- ◆ indicates the total margin available to cover operating expenses
- ◆ reflects product line pricing decisions and/or the impact of purchases/materials on price levels.
- ◆ also an indicator of 'margin performance'
- ◆ Formula - $\dfrac{\text{Sales minus Cost of Goods Sold}}{\text{Sales}} \times 100 = (\%)$

➤ Net Profit (The bottom line)

- ◆ shows after tax profits per $ of sales (%)
- ◆ below standard performance points to weak sales performance or relatively high costs or both
- ◆ also stated as net income or earnings
- ◆ Formula - $\dfrac{\text{Profit after Taxes}}{\text{Sales}} \times 100 = (\%)$

➤ Return on Equity

- ◆ measures the rate of return on a shareholders' investment in the company.
- ◆ does return compensate for risk? (compare to prevailing Government of Canada Bond returns)
- ◆ Formula - $\dfrac{\text{Profit after Taxes} \times 100}{\text{Total Shareholders Equity}} = (\%)$

➢ EBITDA

   ♦ defined as **E**arnings **B**efore **I**nterest, **T**axes, **D**epreciation, and Amortization.

   ♦ indicates the effective cash flow generated by a company on an annual basis.

   ♦ there is a more complex and sophisticated step that uses a ' free cash -flow' measurement. This calculates the company's annual cash flows by including changes in Accounts Receivable, Inventory and Accounts Payable (working capital items). Their use and application is beyond the scope of this text.

2. LIQUIDITY

Liquidity is defined as the ability to meet short-term obligations and measures the relationship between current assets and current liabilities.

➢ Working Capital

   ♦ reveals the balance between liquid assets and claims of short-term creditors.

   ♦ is derived by deducting current liabilities from current assets.

   ♦ Current Ratio   Formula = $\dfrac{\text{Current Assets}}{\text{Current Liabilities}}$

   ♦ A current ratio over 1.5:1 is normally a positive indicator although the nature and relative liquidity of the current assets needs to be considered.

   ♦ The Quick Ratio demonstrates a firm's ability to pay off short-term obligations without reliance on the need to sell inventory.

   ♦ Formula - $\dfrac{\text{Current Assets minus Inventory}}{\text{Current Liabilities}}$

3. STABILITY

➤ Debt to Equity Ratio

- ♦ measures the relationship between debt and equity
- ♦ indicates the extent of funds provided by creditors (debt) and company owners (equity)
- ♦ leverage varies from industry to industry – under 2.5:1 is normally a reasonable comfort zone
- ♦ Formula – $\dfrac{\text{Total Liabilities}}{\text{Total Equity}}$

Note: Intangible assets such as patents, goodwill, etc., should be deducted from the Equity number.

Shareholder loans are sometimes 'subrogated' or 'postponed' to the primary debt holder, which allows this item to be removed from the Liabilities section and added back to Equity thus improving the Debt to Equity ratio.

➤ Total Debt/EBITDA

- ♦ measures the relationship between debt and cash flow – the time frame over which debt is retired from cash flow
- ♦ Formula : $\dfrac{\text{Total Liabilities}}{\text{EBITDA}}$

Note: The EBITDA number is often trimmed back by deducting annual capital expenditures (abbreviated as 'capex') that reoccur on a regular basis. This provides a more accurate indication of cash generation for the year period.

4. DEBT SERVICE

The ability of a company to pay interest and principal on its debt obligations is a key indicator of financial health.

➤ Interest Coverage

- ♦ demonstrates the extent that annual cash flow covers debt interest obligations
- ♦ Formula – $\dfrac{\text{EBITDA}}{\text{Annual Interest}}$

➢ Debt Service Coverage

♦ reveals the extent that annual cash flows cover annual required debt payments (principal and interest)

♦ Formula –

$$\frac{\text{EBITDA}}{\text{Annual Principal and Interest payments}}$$

Note: Annual capital expenditures can also be deducted from the EBITDA number to derive a more accurate cash generation figure.

5. Efficiency

These formulas measure the effective management of working capital items (Accounts Receivable, Inventory, Accounts Payable).

➢ Accounts Receivable collection

♦ Formula - $\frac{\text{Accounts Receivable} \times 365}{\text{Sales}}$

♦ measures the average time (number of days) it takes the business to collect sales made on credit terms

♦ a weak ratio – more than 60 days – points to suspect collection procedures, slow billing or poor credit judgment

➢ Inventory turnover

♦ Formula: $\frac{\text{Cost of Goods Sold}}{\text{Average Inventory}}$

♦ indicates whether the firm has excessive or inadequate inventories. Industry comparisons are required to accurately assess the numbers

♦ slow inventory turnover may point to acceptance of too many quantity discounts or slow moving product lines

➢ Accounts Payable settlement

♦ Formula: $\frac{\text{Accounts Payable} \times 365}{\text{Annual Purchases}}$

♦ indicates the average time (number of days) taken to settle accounts with creditors and suppliers.

♦ points to consider　　– are extended payment terms negotiable?

– are alternative credit sources available?

– are early payment discounts available?

6. GROWTH

These percentages measure the extent and pace of expansion and are usually calculated for Sales, Net Profits, Assets, Debt and Equity.

To assess a company's growth strategy, the following issues must be considered:

➤ What future sales volumes are anticipated as the company expands its product lines and markets?

➤ What levels of profitability and cash generation are forecast and are they sustainable?

➤ What level of bank operating credit is required? Are there seasonal financing needs?

➤ What level of long-term debt is required to finance future capital expenditures and will the company be able to service and repay its increased debt load?

➤ What are the working capital implications of a particular growth strategy and will higher levels of accounts receivable and/or inventories result (uses of cash)?

➤ Can extended payment terms be negotiated with suppliers (sources of cash)?

➤ Can the company raise additional equity? If equity is raised is there a market for minority shares and what percentage ownership stake would be sold and at what price?

➤ Does the company have assets (i.e. real estate) that could be sold or refinanced to raise additional funds?

SOME CONCLUDING COMMENTS ABOUT FINANCIAL RATIOS

➤ Ratio analysis allows you to measure comparative performance over selected time periods.

For example, by comparing the following current ratio, a specific, improving trend can be identified.

2003	2004	2005
2.1	2.4	2.6

It is important to ensure that the same time periods and time of year are used (e.g. comparing the twelve month period ended December 31st, 2004 to December 31st, 2005).

> ➤ Performance in relation to competitor firms can be assessed by obtaining Industry comparables from Dun & Bradstreet and Robert Morris and Associates (RMA) publications.

> > Example – Company ABC current ratio fiscal 2005 = 1.2 (weaker)
> > Industry comparable ratio same year   = 1.8

MANAGING CASH DRIVERS

OVERVIEW

Effective management of short-term assets (cash, accounts receivable, inventories) and short-term sources of financing (accounts payable, bank operating lines) is an important component of the Financial evaluation.

Cash drivers are those management strategies that result in accelerated generation and accumulation of cash resources as part the working capital cycle.

Before detailing the three primary cash drivers, a key distinction needs to be made between *net income* (or profit or earnings) and *net cash flow*.

> ➤ *net income* equals the difference between revenues and expenses.

> ➤ *net cash flow* equals the difference between cash inflows and outflows.

These will invariably be *different*, reflecting:

1. the uneven timing of cash disbursements and the accounting treatment of them.

2. the uneven timing of sales revenues and cash receipts due to delays in account receivable collection.

Due to these timing differences, a company may achieve a strong net profit performance (paper profit) and yet experience a serious cash flow shortfall due to negative cash flows. This section illustrates how a company can improve its net cash flow performance by employing selective cash driver strategies.

THREE PRIMARY CASH DRIVERS

1. IMPROVED ACCOUNTS RECEIVABLE COLLECTION

➤ **Practicing astute credit management**

Establish credit limits for each customer category and use banks or agencies for credit reports. Where appropriate, charge interest on overdue accounts and consider accepting VISA / MasterCard (as opposing to extending credit which may lead to protected repayment).

➤ **Effective Invoicing**

Issue statements at least monthly and ensure that invoices are submitted on the same day goods are shipped. Negotiate front end payments for custom orders.

➤ **Careful Monitoring**

Age receivables by current, 30, 60, and over 90-day categories and place overdue accounts on Cash on Delivery (COD). Monitor and contact overdue accounts on a regular basis

➤ **Prompt Collection**

Establish a formal credit granting and collection policy, including litigation procedures. Wherever possible, negotiate personal guarantees for new and overdue accounts.

2. DEFINED ACCOUNTS PAYABLE SETTLEMENT

➤ Age payables into Current, 30, 60 days and over 90-day categories.

➤ Extend terms with key suppliers, especially to mirror seasonal cash needs. However, if attractive early payment discounts are offered, take advantage of them.

3. MAXIMIZE INVENTORY TURNOVER

➤ Return or sell off outdated or obsolete merchandise.

➤ Determine the number of times your major product lines turn each year. How does this compare to industry averages? The faster the inventory turnover, the greater the cash flow.

➤ Are shrinkage control procedures in place (to guard against goods slipping out of the back door)?

➤ Are re-order policies in place based on past inventory levels and target turnover numbers?

> ➤ Are the 'costs' of carrying inventory known (i.e. interest and handling costs)?

> ➤ Do you have alternative sources of supply (i.e. improved delivery terms)?

> ➤ Determine which 20% of your customers contribute to 80% of your sales.

Figure 3-2 (below) illustrates the inter-relationship between the primary cash drivers – Inventory Turnover, Accounts Receivable collection and Accounts Payable settlement.

Reduced days in Inventory (**A**) and Accounts Receivable (**B**) allied with lengthened days in Accounts Payable (**C**) indicates the relative success of the company's cash driver strategies.

Figure 3-1

Cash Driver Relationships

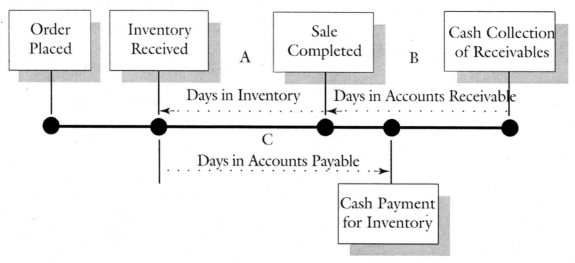

Source: Adapted from *Short Term Financial Management* by Maness & Zietlow. Copyright ©1997, The Dryden Press, reproduced with permission of the publisher.

OTHER CASH DRIVER STRATEGIES

> ➤ Increases in property values (appraisal values versus net book value on the Balance Sheet) may allow refinancing and generate surplus cash (working capital) to finance expansion.

> ➤ Consider leasing out under-utilized assets to third parties.

> ➤ Borrow *short term* for short term needs and borrow *long term* for longer term needs. Match the amortization of the loan with the expected useful life of the asset.

OPTIMIST™ FINANCIAL MODELING SOFTWARE[1]

DESCRIPTION

Optimist™ is a leading edge financial management tool developed in Australia, which uses historical accounting data to:

- ➤ Evaluate and analyze past performance.

- ➤ Develop strategy for business operations' future financial and growth performance.

Key drivers in the Income Statement and Balance Sheet are compared to determine what impact they will have on working capital and operating results.

Operating strategies are reviewed from two innovative perspectives:

1. From a 'What If' perspective – what if sales increased by 15%, what would be the impact on other related financial variables?

2. From a 'Goal Seek' perspective – setting a Net Cash Income target of say, $100K and then investigating which cash drivers/variables would combine to achieve the desired results. For example:

    - ♦ Reducing days Receivable
    - ♦ Reducing days Inventory
    - ♦ Increasing days Payable
    - ♦ Increasing Price
    - ♦ Reducing COGS
    - ♦ Reducing operating expenses

(A detailed analysis of the Optimist™ software is to be found in G. Pazmandy Business modeling (3rd Edition) Tekniks Publications Pty Ltd, Sydney Australia ISBN 0 9578152 0 4 Chapter 8: pages 215-257).

APPLICATION

Optimist is used extensively by CEO's to focus on their financial growth potential and by commercial banks to understand their clients' ability to generate sustainable cash flow to repay bank and other creditors debt.

A major benefit of Optimist is that it analyses how well a company can service debt via the 'Profit to Cash' report which shows the historical flow of cash through the business and the resultant Net Cash Income. If this is positive, the business has generated sufficient cash flow to fund operations as well as pay taxes, interest and dividends.

FINANCIAL PROJECTIONS

OVERVIEW

Up to this point, *historical* financial information has allowed us to diagnose financial health and performance. An equally important element of the evaluation process is the completion of financial *forecasts;* in essence, the creation of a financial road map that enables company management to foresee where they are going. This process is particularly important if you are seeking increased bank financing or additional sources of equity.

The following section details three key documents that comprise a comprehensive financial forecast:

1. Pro Forma (Projected) Income Statements
2. Projected Balance Sheet
3. Cash Flow Budget

1. PRO FORMA INCOME STATEMENTS

The process:

> - Should cover three to five years into the future.
> - The first two years should include complete quarterly income projections, thereafter annually.
> - Projected revenues should be based on historical and anticipated sales performance.
> - The revenue forecast should be derived from either
>   - market size *multiplied by* estimated % market share *multiplied by* estimated growth rate
>
>   or
>
>   - percentage growth based on historical performance (i.e. 10% sales growth over the next three years, etc.)

Note: Industry data on market size and growth can reveal how your marketplace is changing as opposed to reliance on your own internal numbers.

> - *Cost of Goods Sold (COGS)* forecast should be based on prevailing industry gross profit margins.
>
> - *Sales, General and Administration (SGA)* expenses represent company overhead. If revenues are forecast to grow beyond a fixed or relevant range, use an SGA to Revenue ratio to ensure support costs grow in tandem with revenues.

> *Interest Expense* should be based on forecast levels of long-term financing.

> *Taxes and Depreciation* forecasts would be based on prevailing tax rates and depreciation allowances.

2. PROJECTED BALANCE SHEET

The process:

> Three-year outlook: derived from historic ratio analysis and your pro forma Income Statement

> Projected Accounts Receivable, Inventory, and Accounts Payable: can be derived from historic ratios and forecast revenues/costs/purchases.

> Fixed Assets: need to reflect any future significant capital expenditures in the future.

> Equity: would reflect any new source of capital and ongoing buildup of retained earnings from forecast net profits (after dividend payout).

> Balancing Item: will be either cash or bank operating debt

Note: It is crucial to document any assumptions regarding the financial ratios.

3. CASH FLOW BUDGET

Will project up to three years out, with the first year calculated on a monthly basis. This process highlights the importance of timing differences in cash receipts and disbursements.

Cash In

> Utilize the Projected Income Statement and convert revenue forecasts into cash receipts by month.

> Review the Account Receivable listing to determine actual payment terms taken (i.e., 20% of receivables paid in 90 days. Therefore – 20% of January sales are not received until April.)

> Other cash receipts would include:

  ♦ supplier rebates
  ♦ new bank loans
  ♦ cash injections from new shareholders

Cash Out

> Three main items

♦ Overhead expenses: fixed costs like rent, salaries, heat and power.

♦ Cash outlays for purchases (inventory) and for direct labor.

♦ Intermittent expenses: loan payments, capex, dividends, tax payments.

Remember:

> Assembly of the 'cash in' and 'cash out' data allows the completion of a 12 month cash flow forecast which determines the cash position on a monthly basis and resultant short term borrowing or investment requirements.

> Clearly document assumptions.

> Contrast to actual performance thereby highlighting the impact of your cash driver performance.

> The cash flow budget is an effective early warning system especially when negative variances between actual and forecast month-end cash positions emerge.

> It also indicates to a bank or investor that you understand the operations and cash drivers for your business. Month by month presentation is crucial, enabling you to react quickly to shortfalls or significant variances.

A NOTE ON SENSITIVITY ANALYSIS
(Also known as 'what-if' analysis or 'stress testing')

Spreadsheet software allows certain key assumptions (sales growth, gross profit margin, account receivable collection, etc.) to be altered.

Different scenarios can then be generated and presented on a best case/expected case/worst case basis, usually over the first year period.

Example:

A hotel is planning to expand operations by constructing a new wing and doubling the available number of hotel rooms. To secure the necessary construction and long term financing, a series of financial projections are prepared with different scenarios presented as to percentage occupancy, average room rates and variable costs.

The lenders can also apply their own sensitivity analysis to the scenarios and calculate a break even point versus debt service requirements; i.e., term loan payments are covered at 1.25 times when a 65% occupancy and a 25% drop in average room rates is simulated. The lender then has to consider if this is a reasonable worst-case scenario.

BREAK-EVEN ANALYSIS

All organizations incur various costs in order to operate. Generally those costs can be broken down into two categories, fixed costs and variable costs.

Fixed costs: are costs that, in total, remain much the same over some relevant range of activity levels. For example, office rent will stay the same over the year no matter what level of service provided. Additional examples of fixed costs include salaries (as distinct from wages), property taxes, depreciation expenses, and lease costs.

Variable costs: are costs that vary with activity volume changes. These costs can generally be expressed as cost per unit or as a percentage of revenue.

Example: It takes a certain amount of dollars worth of materials (paper, ink, labour wages) to produce a book. If the variable cost of producing a book is $10, a print run of 100 books would incur variable costs of $1,000 while a run of 1,000 books would incur variable costs of $10,000.

Some costs can be semi-variable, or semi-fixed.

Example: If a retail outlet in a shopping mall pays $1,000 per month rent plus 5% of monthly gross sales, the $1,000 is fixed and 5% of each month's sales amount paid is variable. Electricity costs and a salary plus 'commissions' compensation plans are other examples of semi-variable costs.

Break-even analysis is a managerial technique that separates costs into fixed and variable components. At a certain level of activity, revenues are equal to the total costs, fixed plus variable. At that level of activity, the organization is at *its break-even point*. It has covered all its costs but has not made a profit or surplus.

Exhibit I (next page) provides a graphical view of break-even analysis and indicates the break-even point.

The total fixed costs are fixed over a range of activity volume (units), as indicated by the horizontal line. In addition, each unit sold incurs a variable cost. As volume increases, the total variable costs increase. *The break-even point is where total revenues equal total costs and is indicated by the point where the revenues line intersects with the total costs line.*

Point A at the bottom of the graph shows the volume level in activity units required to be sold in order to break-even.

BREAK-EVEN CHART

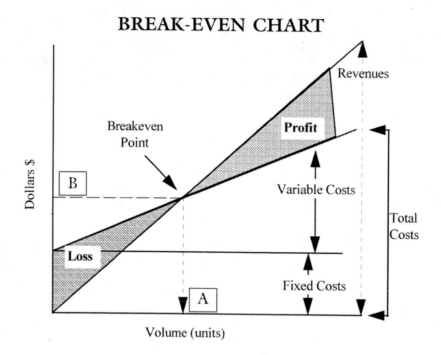

Point B indicates the dollar amount of revenues required to break-even. If the number of units sold exceeds the volume at the break-even point, a profit or surplus is generated. Alternatively, if the number of units fails to meet the break-even volume, a loss or deficit occurs.

CONTRIBUTION ANALYSIS

Contribution margin is the amount left over from an activity unit's sale after covering its variable cost. This remaining contribution then goes to cover fixed costs. Therefore, selling price (SP) minus unit variable cost (UVC) equals unit contribution margin (UCM).

Example: If a book is sold for $100 and has a variable cost of $60, the difference of $40 is the unit contribution margin (UCM) available to cover total fixed costs.

If total fixed costs are $10,000, it will take $10,000 divided by the $40 UCM or 250 books to break-even. Each and every book sold contributes $40 towards fixed costs. If more than 250 books are sold, each book sold over the 250 break-even volume, contributes $40 to profit (surplus). Thus if 300 books are sold, the organization has a profit (surplus) of $2,000 ($40 UCM x 50 units over break-even).

Understanding this concept allows us to change any of the items and assess the impact.

For example, if we thought that variable costs would rise to $65 and we wanted to earn a profit (surplus) of $4,000, we can easily calculate the impact:

SP	$100
UVC	65
UCM	35

- Fixed costs + desired profit = $14,000 ($10,000 + $4,000)

- $14,000/$35 = 400 books need to be sold to meet our objective.

- This translates into $40,000 in revenues (400 books x $100 selling price).

Another approach is on a percentage basis. The UCM is 35% of the SP. By dividing the amount required to be covered ($14,000) by .35 we arrive at the required $40,000 figure.

KEY POINTS

- The lower the break-even point, the less vulnerable the firm to unexpected cost increases.

- The more costs that can be made 'variable' (i.e., occur only once a sale is made) the better.

- Strive to keep contribution (gross profit) margin high and break-even point low.

- Minimize fixed costs.

CAPITAL BUDGETING

Capital budgeting allows a company owner to make financial decisions about long-term investments. Some examples of capital budgeting decisions are:

- Replacement of company's fleet of vehicles with new models.

- Development of a new product line that will require extensive R&D and commercialization.

- Purchase of land parcel and the construction of a new commercial building.

- Purchase of manufacturing and/or computer equipment.

KEY QUESTION

"Do the future benefits from the investment exceed the costs of making the investment?"

Three different techniques can be used to determine the future benefits with each one answering a specific question.

1. ACCOUNTING RETURN ON INVESTMENT

Question: What average dollar profits are generated per average? investment dollar?

Calculation: $\dfrac{\text{Average annual after tax profit per year}}{\text{Average book value of investment}} = \%$

Example:

New equipment costs $20,000, depreciated over four years to final year (zero salvage value). Average net book value is $10,000.

Expected after tax profits

Year	After tax profit
1	$2,000
2	$4,000
3	$5,000
4	$6,000

Average expected profits over the four year period = $4,250

Accounting return on investment = $\dfrac{\$4,250}{\$10,000} = 42.5\%$

SHORTCOMINGS

- ➤ Based on accounting profits rather than actual cash flows.

- ➤ Ignores the time value of money

- ➤ Company owners' minimum acceptable return (hurdle rate) needs to be established in order to determine acceptance or rejection of the project.

2. PAY BACK PERIOD

Question: How long will it take to recover the original investment?

Calculation: New equipment costs $45,000 with an expected life of 10 years and is depreciated on a straight-line basis at $4,500 per year.

Expected After Tax Cash Flows

Year	After Tax Profit	Depreciation	After Tax Cash Flow
1 to 2	$3,000	+ $4,500	= $7,500
3 to 6	$6,000	+ $4,500	= $10,500
7 to 10	$7,500	+ $4,500	= $11,000

The pay back period will be approx. **4.9** years and is derived by allocating the cumulative annual cash flows against the original $45,000 investment

STRENGTHS

➤ Does give an indication of risk – the longer the pay back period, the greater the risk.

WEAKNESSES

➤ Does not consider the time value of money

➤ Does not consider financial impact of cash flows received after pay back period

3. DISCOUNTED CASH FLOW

Question: How does the present value of future benefits arising from the investment compare with the present-day cost of the investment?

Discount Cash Flow (DCF) techniques are complex. Two analytical methods can be utilized.

NET PRESENT VALUE (NPV)

The original cash outlay is compared to the value of future cash flows discounted back to the present using a predetermined rate of return (discount rate). If the NPV is positive, then the project is acceptable.

INTERNAL RATE OF RETURN (IRR)

The rate of return that is derived where the present value of the cost of the investment equals the present value of future cash flows.

USEFUL WEB SITES

www.fool.com	Motley Fool web site: refer to the Rule Maker and Rule Breaker sections where financial and strategic bench marks are presented.
www.rmahq.org	RMA annual statement studies providing comparative financial ratio data(subscription required) *Note:* these reports can also be accessed through your local commercial banker.
www.americanexpress.com	Small Business – Business Resources section

Notes from text.

1. www.inmatrix.com.au

CHAPTER 4
MARKETING STRATEGY

OVERVIEW

There tends to be much confusion about what 'marketing' is. Many business people think that marketing is selling or that it can be summarized by the 4 P's of marketing – price, product, promotion and place (distribution). While these items are encompassed by marketing, there is much more to this critical area of business.

OUR DEFINITION

Marketing is a set of market-related activities that analyzes the marketplace, develops a market-driven strategy and executes that strategy. These activities allow a company to provide targeted customers with a portfolio of products and services that add customer value and meet unfulfilled customer needs.

Our presentation will be segmented as follows:

1. Preliminary Analysis

2. Portfolio Assessment

3. Strategy Execution

This framework is summarised in the following diagram.

Marketing Strategy

Stage 1

Stage 2

Stage 3

Preliminary Analysis

Portfolio Assessment

Strategy Execution

Preliminary Analysis	Portfolio Assessment	Strategy Execution
1. Situation Analysis	1. Specific Competitive Threats	1. Communicating the Vision
2. Product or Service Review	2. Pricing Considerations	2. Development of Skills & Competencies
3. Market Segment Assessment	3. Product Mix Issues	3. Establishing Incentives
4. Unmet Customer Needs	4. Placement (Distribution) Channels	4. Acquiring Resources
5. Competitor Evaluation	5. Promotion Requirements	5. Development of the Appropriate Organization Structure
6. Competitive Advantage	6. People Needs	6. Build a Customer Relationship Management Strategy
	7. Partnering Opportunities	
	8. Financial Feasibility	
	9. Business Retention & Trust Building	
	10. Business Development & Prospecting	

1. PRELIMINARY ANALYSIS

Completion of a careful preliminary analysis is the first stage in crafting a comprehensive marketing strategy. There are six steps to this process:

A. SITUATION ANALYSIS

This will involve a brief documentation process using the following headings (the PEST and Industry areas have been covered in detail in Chapters 1 and 2).

- Brief History of Organization
- External Opportunities and Threats (PEST)
- Industry overview (Five Forces)
- Internal environment – Strengths & Weaknesses

B. PRODUCT OR SERVICES REVIEW

- A listing of current Products/Services should be completed
- The potential for new 'follow-on' product /services initiatives?
- Market/Product related challenges and issues
- Features and Benefits
- Product adoption behaviours – what triggers the buying decision?

C. MARKET SEGMENT ASSESSMENT

You need to identify and define:
- Market segments in size (dollars and units) and estimated growth rates
- Segment criteria can include:
  - Geographical
  - Industry
  - Demographics
  - Procurement based
  - Operational needs

Estimated share of market segment should also be identified.

A Market segment can be defined as: groups of customers and potential customers who have similar needs and desires, which are distinct from other segments and can be targeted as a group by adopting unique marketing strategies

You then need to assess:

> Future trends for each segment and customer needs and wants in each segment?

> Are there primary, secondary, or even tertiary segments? In other words, who is the real customer?

And also understand:

> How or where do segment customers purchase your products or services?

> The profit potential of each segment?

D.   UNMET CUSTOMER NEEDS?

In order to identify unmet customers' needs, consider the following:

> What new needs could be derived from your development of new technology, processes, or equipment?

> Will new environmental regulations create new opportunities?

> Do new PEST factor create any further opportunities?

> Are there any opportunities for increasing value-added products and services?

A NOTE ON MARKET RESEARCH

A key component in identifying unmet customer needs is undertaking a market research process, which would involve completion of the following steps:

> Define the marketing issues and the objectives of the research project. What do you want to get out of the project?

> Develop a research plan: What types of resources are available? What are the expected outcomes? What research approach will be used? How will research participants be identified and contacted as part of the Primary research process?

> Data Collection: It is critical to ensure that the data collected is unbiased to maintain validity. Care must be taken to exclude interviewer bias or questionable answers.

➤ Data Analysis: Once data is collected, a wide variety of statistical and summary techniques can be used to interpret it. These techniques should have been identified in the research plan.

➤ Draw conclusions: These will lead to the identification of specific customer wants, needs and will assist in pinpointing target segments. Such conclusions must be logically derived from the research findings.

➤ Secondary research can use external sources such as Statistics Canada, industry associations or purchased marketing research from external research firms. However, you must still do the majority of the analysis yourself in order to draw specific conclusions about your existing or potential products and services.

E. COMPETITOR EVALUATION

When analyzing competitors from a marketing perspective, you need to consider the following broad issues:

➤ What is the estimated market share of competitors, categorized by your primary product/service offering categories? List the competitors in order of their relative current impact

➤ Endeavor to assess competitor financial resources, product quality, service and pricing strategies.

➤ Review their competing technology attributes (intellectual property protection) and channels of distribution.

F. COMPETITIVE ADVANTAGE

The next step is to ask yourself – do you have a sustainable competitive advantage?

You probably do if you meet the following criteria:

➤ Competitors find it difficult to imitate your products or services.

➤ You have access to a diverse set of market segments.

➤ You contribute in a significant way to customers' perceived value of the product or service offered.

Sustainable competitive advantages are generally derived through factors like lower costs, higher quality, added value and specific advantages such as a geographic monopoly, franchise strength or brand image.

A NOTE ON COMPETITIVE INTELLIGENCE

Competitive intelligence (CI) is a proactive and structured approach in gathering information about competitors' market related activities. In building a defined C I. strategy, the identification and databasing of specific information is a key process – such information would include current pricing initiatives, trade shows and conferences, recruitment drives, online databases, magazines, and product catalogs.

There are some key ethical considerations; the information to be gathered has to be publicly available as opposed to the engagement in clandestine, undercover activities.

Another key element to an effective C I. strategy is properly structured internal communications where 'early warnings' on competitor activities are monitored on a regular basis.

An effective CI process enables the company to more effectively guage its relative competitive advantage.

2. PORTFOLIO ASSESSMENT

Having completed the Preliminary Market Analysis, we now move on to the Portfolio Assessment stage – where growth initiatives are charted for each discrete product or service.

For example, consider an upscale resort based on Vancouver Island (west coast) that offers a selection of services offerings to discrete market segments, which might be classified as follows:

PRODUCT OFFERING	MARKET SEGMENT
Accommodation and food services	♦ Business traveler ♦ Week end getaways
Conferences	♦ Business sector ♦ Government sector
Weddings	♦ Local ♦ Out of province
Tours	♦ Golf ♦ Ecotourism

For this particular client, it is apparent that are 4 separate service offerings each with two discrete market segments. Thus, there will be eight separate product/market portfolios that will need to be assessed using the following 10-step process:

HEADINGS

Product/ service description

The specific product or service offering will be detailed here i.e. Conferences

Target Market segment

The specific market segment for the product/service offering will be identified here i.e. Government sector

Market positioning statement

For each product/service offered (or to be offered), a Market Positioning Statement should be developed that captures the 'brand image' in the minds of Customers and other related stakeholders.

1) SPECIFIC COMPETITIVE THREATS

Need to be considered for each portfolio item:

- Can you assess the market share of competitors? Have there been any market share changes over the past few years? Why did the changes occur?

- Is there potential for competitive actions and reactions to any new product or service introductions?

- At what stage is the market segment on the product/service life cycle?

2) PRICING CONSIDERATIONS

A price should be set that communicates *value* to your targeted customers. In pricing your product offerings, complete the following assessment process:

- What is the overall objective? Is it to build market share? Maximize revenues? Maximize profits? Achieve product quality leadership?

- What are the product costs at different volumes? What is the average gross margin?

➤ How do your prices compare to competitors' prices?

➤ Have you considered potential for volume/segment discounts?

➤ What will be the impact of transportation costs, handling and insurance?

➤ Are there any privacy policy implications (need to clearly state how customer information will be administered)?

3) Product mix issues

➤ Have you designed and developed products and services so that the targeted customers can easily identify, understand and determine the value that is delivered to them?

➤ Is there a need for some form of visual representation (photos, drawings, etc.)?

➤ Are you generating at least one new product/service development ahead of the marketplace?

➤ Is there a clear description of supporting customer service(s) needed?

➤ Are there warranty implications (what is covered, timing, who will support, etc.)?

➤ What are the packaging requirements and designs, if any?

4) Placement (Distribution) channels

Trade analysis is the analysis of the distribution channels. Consider the following:

➤ How do you plan to distribute your products and services? How do your competitors distribute their products and services?

➤ Are there other potential distribution channel options?

➤ Where is value added in the 'market chain'? Market chain refers to the complete channel from making the product to the ultimate purchase by the final consumer.

➤ How and where does your company add value in the market chain?

➤ How and where do your competitors add value in the market chain?

➤ Can you partner with appropriate suppliers or distributors to increase value?

5) PROMOTION REQUIREMENTS

- Do you advertise and promote your product and services in places (trade shows) that your target audiences frequent and in a manner consistent with the feeling and perceptions that your products and services have created.

- Promotion includes advertising, direct marketing, e-marketing, sales promotions, and public relations for both your firm and product offerings.

- What is the current amount of promotion budget?

- What major message theme(s) is required for integrated marketing communications (desired positioning)?

- Is there personal selling required (type and number of salespeople, training incentives, compensation)?

- Are there web site development issue and initiatives to consider?
    - Has your web site be optimized for search engine marketing?
    - Is your content being refreshed on a regular basis? (Many companies build their web sites and then update them only once a year).
    - Do you have an 'outbound' email strategy to keep customers up-to-date on new specials, promos etc. using an opt-in email list?

6) PEOPLE NEEDS

- What are the staffing requirements to position and then sell the product/ service into the appropriate market segment?

- Are there training and compensation issues to address?

- Have teams been set up by product function and /or market segment?

7) PARTNERING OPPORTUNITIES

- Is there potential for a strategic alliance, licensing arrangement or joint venture to share the costs of market development?

- What due diligence steps need to be taken to ensure compatibility?

8) FINANCIAL FEASIBILITY

For existing products/services:

> What are the forecast revenues and contribution for the next fiscal year?

> Has a sensitivity analysis been performed – best, expected, worst – case?

For new products/services:

> What are the variable and fixed start-up costs and the projected break-even?

9) BUSINESS RETENTION & TRUST BUILDING

For existing clients:

> Ensure there is a clear 'client retention' focus – to guard the back door,

> Explore ways to 'cross-sell' other products/services.

> Continuously build trust and request client testimonials and referrals

10) BUSINESS DEVELOPMENT AND PROSPECTING

For new clients and prospects:

> Develop a formal prospecting system using a 'sales funnel' process.

> Build a prospect database and develop a 'qualification pipeline'

> Plan and act strategically – have your team adapt the mindset that they have been hired, on a contract basis, to build market share in a specific business vertical.

> Understand the Pareto 80:20 rule – for example, 80% of contribution margin comes from 20% of clients

> Consider alliances/relationships with industry associations.

> Build a database of key supporters and referral sources.

> Portray yourself as an 'alternate service provider' and friendly sounding board to those 'happy for now' prospects.

To assist this rigorous process, we have developed a useful template that can be used for the Product/Market portfolio assessment – see below:

Product/Service description

Target Market segment

Market Positioning statement

Portfolio Assessment

Steps	Issues to consider?
1) Competitive threats	
2) Pricing considerations	
3) Product mix issues	
4) Placement channels	
5) Promotion requirements	
6) People needs	
7) Partnering opportunities?	
8) Financial feasibility	
9) Business retention & trust building	
10) Business development & prospecting	

3. MARKET STRATEGY EXECUTION

Once the market analysis and portfolio positioning process has been completed, the agreed-upon initiatives and tactics must now be executed.

A solid execution or implementation plan requires the following:

COMMUNICATION OF THE VISION

It is important to ensure that company personnel buy into your company's market vision and its products and services.

DEVELOPMENT OF SKILLS AND COMPETENCIES

You need to assess what skills your people need to executive the vision? Do they have them now? Can they be developed? Can you acquire them?

ESTABLISHING INCENTIVES

Proper incentives are required to motivate your people to perform the required market- driven tasks and initiatives. Lack of proper incentives will lead to slower execution and change. Incentives can be either financial or non-financial.

ACQUIRING RESOURCES

The execution of a market strategy cannot be successfully accomplished without having the necessary resources to implement the plan. A lack of required resources (such as the appropriate people, financing, strategic partners) causes frustration and lack of motivation.

DEVELOPMENT OF THE APPROPRIATE ORGANIZATION STRUCTURE.

An appropriate market-oriented structure needs to be set up with clearly defined lines of authority and responsibility in place.

The structure should be linked to key success factors that have been developed by the various departments and divisions within the firm. These 'responsibility units' will be motivated by specific accomplishment targets that have been agreed upon.

BUILD A CUSTOMER RELATIONSHIP MANAGEMENT STRATEGY

It is critical that a formal system is in place to manage customer relationships which involves not just the installation of appropriate I.T infrastructure but the training of employees who are guided by a strategic process to acquire, service, cross sell and retain clients.

USEFUL WEB SITES

www.marketingsherpa.com	Case studies in sales and marketing for companies selling into internet markets
www.strategymag.com	Canadian marketing report with a focus on information-based marketing
www.forrester.com	Leading independent research firm with some free information
www.crmmarketplace.com	Sourcing site for CRM professionals
www.researchinfo.com	Market Research roundtable
www.fuld.com	Competitive intelligence guide
www.wilsonweb.com/research	Internet Marketing information with many free articles in the research section.

NOTES

CHAPTER 5
THE OPERATIONS REVIEW

OVERVIEW

The manner in which a business conducts its basic operations is an important element in the Size-Up process. In this section, the following six key areas of operations management will be covered:

- **Process** management
- **Facilities** management
- **Inventory** management
- **Quality** management
- **Risk** management
- **Project** management

In addition, we also review:

- Legal considerations
- Business technology, ecommerce and website issues.

In their simplest form, operations consist of the completion of activities that are necessary to get the task performed. The operations process transforms inputs into outputs. The end result is the successful delivery of a product or service that meets customers' quality requirements and expectations.

A key outcome of this function is the improved productivity of the company, which allows it to compete more effectively in its marketplace. Generally organizations with higher productivity possess a superior competitive advantage.

Operations are not an isolated function. They are closely intertwined with the other functional areas of the business – especially finance, marketing and human resources.

PRODUCTS VERSUS SERVICES

Implications:

- ➤ Service firms have greater direct customer contact. Individuals providing services normally have more face-to-face contact with customers than those individuals performing manufacturing operations.

- ➤ Product manufacturing operations can build or deplete product inventories to meet demand cycles whereas service providers cannot "store up" their services. They have to adopt strategies that level out the demand process.

- ➤ Quality standards are more difficult to establish and measure in service operations.

- ➤ Productivity is generally easier to measure in production operations.

PROCESS MANAGEMENT

1. What type of production process is employed?

   Consider the following types of manufacturing processes:
   - ◆ Assembly line: work is broken down into small repetitive tasks. This process involves long production runs and is usually associated with large manufacturing companies (e.g., car assembly plant).
   - ◆ Batch flow: intermediate type of production involving more variety and less volume than an assembly line. Less variety and more volume than job shops (e.g., bottling plant – different drink varieties).
   - ◆ Job shop: short production runs. One or only few products are produced before shifting to a different production setup. Involves general purpose equipment and workforce with each job usually unique (e.g. machine shops, printing companies).
   - ◆ Just in time: parts go through each manufacturing step driven by a daily demand pull schedule which reduces inventories and speeds up the response time.

2. How does the production process relate to the firm's marketing strategies?

3. What types of equipment and technologies are being used? Are any changes required or planned in order to remain competitive?

FACILITIES MANAGEMENT

Facilities can be defined as a company's physical settings, support services and infrastructure – which must be utilized to support business processes and strategic objectives.

A key question is – how does the occupying business secure maximum benefit from its facilities?

Some issues to consider:

➤ What is the capacity of the facility and how close is current output to that capacity?

➤ Are there any plans to increase capacity? What are the associated costs?

➤ Is production/service delivery planning a difficult task? Is demand difficult to estimate?

➤ What are the near term capital expenditure (capex) requirements?

➤ Is there potential to outsource certain elements of facilities services?

LOCATION OF PHYSICAL FACILITIES

The location decision for a company owner is an important one and can range from operating a home office to purchasing, leasing or renting a commercial building.

There are five key factors in determining an appropriate location:

1) *Financial*

Cost of land and improvements.

Current property leases.

Local labour costs and tax structures.

2) *Personal Preferences*

> Proximity to home.

> Colleagues, friends, or relatives close by.

3) *Market Access*

> Convenience for clients and suppliers.

> Proximity to target markets.

4) *Resource availability*

> Accessibility to raw materials.

> Effective transportation links and communications.

> Qualified labor force and management.

5) *Environmental Conditions*

> Local laws and regulatory structure. Government support and incentives.

> Climate.

> Quality of life.

HOME OFFICES

Many small companies commence operations as home-based businesses. This decision is usually driven by cost considerations and the fact that business is in an early growth stage. There are obvious advantages with a home-based business scenario but such arrangements may not work for everyone.

Potential downsides:

- Client demands and expectations. Working from home can lead to longer response times, especially if colleagues are in separate locations.

- Adverse zoning by-laws.

- Lack of focus. Too many distractions from family and neighborhood.

- Difficulty in maintaining spatial boundaries between business and home.

HOME SHORING

An increasing number of companies are are seeking a less contentious alternative to call centres in Asia. Known as "home-shoring". Employees are based in their own homes, as part of a virtual call centre. Using the same technology that makes outsourcing abroad possible, calls are routed to a different destination – the employees' home.

Industry research estimates there are more than 100,000 home-based agents in the US with increases in productivity, lower costs and lower attrition being achieved in these virtual call centres.[1]

INCUBATORS

Business incubators provide early stage entrepreneurs with affordable space, clerical assistance, and, sometimes, mentorship facilities. Many are funded by government agencies and/or universities and appear to be a growing trend.

Benefits include:

➤ Access to legal and /accounting services.

➤ Profile and credibility.

➤ Access to investing 'angels' and venture capital sources.

LEASE OR BUY

Early stage companies invariably lease premises and often commence operations by renting space on a short-term (month-to-month) basis before entering into longer term and more formalized lease arrangements.

Advantages to leasing (for both established companies and start-ups):

➤ Preservation of capital for other uses. While this is somewhat obvious for start-ups, many established companies fail to recognize the significant impact that a property purchase decision will have on their working capital and future potential.

Example:

Company XYZ purchases a commercial property for $1 million and obtains $600,000 in long-term financing (with loan payments equivalent to lease payments) and the balance of the purchase funded by $400,000 in cash.

The $400,000 cash outflow *reduces* the company's working capital resources. (These funds could have been used to identify additional markets and then launch a new generation of product lines providing enhanced revenue and earnings performance).

> ➤ Greater flexibility: Ability to relocate at the end of the lease term and find larger premises, if necessary.

> ➤ Fluctuations in local property values (especially decreases in market values) do not affect the value of the company.

Advantages of buying

> ➤ Able to modify or customize property.

> ➤ No third party relationship to landlord.

> ➤ May enjoy property value appreciation.

> ➤ Surplus space could be leased out.

INVENTORY MANAGEMENT

The effective management of inventories is a critical component of business operations and can often mean the difference between success and failure, especially in smaller retail or wholesale firms where inventories represents a major financial investment.

1. What type of inventory is carried (raw materials, work in process, finished goods)?

2. What is the makeup of each type of inventory and how significant is each?

3. How are inventories managed with a focus on controlling costs?

Techniques include:

The ABC method – involves the classification of inventory into three categories, A,B,C, based upon their respective cost value. Managerial focus is applied to the most expensive and important 'A' items.

Just-in-time inventory system – items are received 'just as' the last item of that product type moves from inventory and is put into service. This process involves very close co-operation with suppliers to ensure that they can deliver materials quickly and in a highly predictable manner

Economic Order Quantity – this process involves a focus on minimizing high ordering and high carrying costs.

Consider the following inventory management objectives:

> - Minimize inventory investment by carrying smaller inventories, which result in lower financing, storage, and obsolescence costs.

> - Keep work in process on schedule.

> - Maximizing sales and product selection (keeping sufficient inventory to avoid stock outs and missed sales opportunities).

> - Guarding against deterioration, shrinkage or theft.

Is there potential to use RFID technology?

Radio Frequency Identification (RFID) is an *automatic identification* method, consisting of storage and remote retrieval data using devices called RFID tags which can be attached to products, either held in inventory or in process of delivery. Wal-Mart makes extensive use of this technology in tracking its merchandise flow.

TOTAL QUALITY MANAGEMENT

Product and service quality are critical success factors to ensure survival in today's highly competitive business environment. The concept of Total Quality Management (TQM) denotes a comprehensive, holistic approach in providing high quality products and services that meet customer needs.

SOME KEY POINTS TO CONSIDER

> - How are customer expectations managed? – it is critical to understand client needs and 'satisfaction drivers' when crafting a TQM strategy within a business
> - How important is production/service *delivery* quality?
> - Has a clearly defined 'organizational culture' been developed where there is an unrelenting focus on quality issues?

Initiatives like *continuous improvement* (a constant effort to improve product/service quality) and *benchmarking* (studying the best practices of competing firms) can be utilized to meet such needs.

> Are there any product return policies or warranty implications?

> Is it possible to obtain international recognition of the firm's quality management programs by meeting a series of standards known as ISO 9000?

> Developing TQM techniques and tools that will assist in building a defined quality management program. Examples follow:

Employee participation – for example, *quality circles* which involve regular meetings to identify, analyze and resolve work-related problems.

Developing *inspection standards* which define a desired quality level and allowable tolerances.

Statistical process control – one of the best-known techniques today is Six Sigma, which is being increasingly adopted to improve process quality.

Six Sigma offers a structured and distinct method to reduce defects and wastage, which can often account for a significant percentage of sales revenue.

Six Sigma is a registered trademark of Motorola Inc. which implemented the technique in the 1980s. 'Sigma' is the Greek letter that denotes standard deviation – a Six Sigma organization is striving to achieve just 3.4 defects per million.

Jack Welsh, former CEO of General Electric, is a huge fan of Six Sigma and defines it as a quality program that improves customers experience, lowers costs and builds 'sticky' relationships with customers. It is seen as a method to eliminate unpleasant surprises and broken promises.[2]

To work on an existing process, which needs improvement, the 'DMAIC' approach would be used:

Define – the process goals in terms of key critical quality parameters

Measure – the current process performance in context of goals

Analyze – the current situation in terms of causes of variations and defects

Improve – the process by systematically reducing variation and eliminating defects

Control – the future performance of the process[3]

The DMAIC Approach

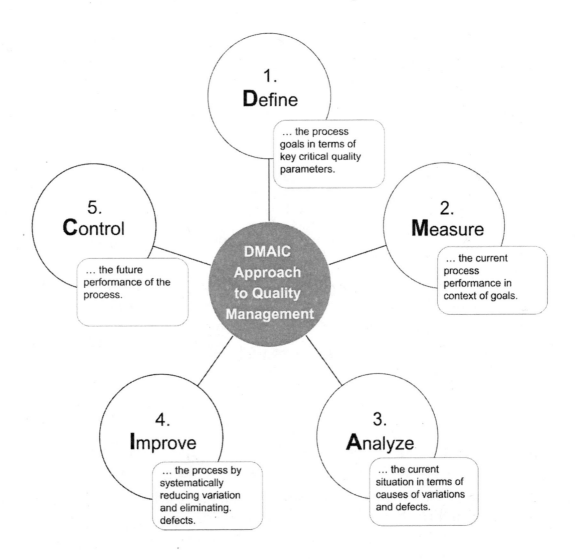

RISK MANAGEMENT

Risk management (managing risk factors) involves the implementation of programs that preserve assets and the earning power of the business. Insurance protection is an integral part of a sound risk management program. In conjunction with an insurance professional, the following steps should be completed in evaluating potential risks facing your business:

1) Identify which business risks need to be insured.

   These will fall into three categories:

> ➤ Property risks

> ➤ Personnel risks

> ➤ Customer risks

2) Coverage should be limited to major potential losses. Determine the size of loss that could be handled without serious financial difficulty.

3) Relate premium costs to the relative probability of loss.

MAJOR TYPES OF BUSINESS INSURANCE

Commercial Property Insurance: Covers damages resulting from fire, storm, theft and other dangers. Many policies cover 'all risks'(any damage that is not specifically excluded).

General Liability Insurance: Is usually combined with property coverage in a standard business owners' policy and covers legal defense costs if someone is injured on your property or by your product.

Auto Insurance: Comprehensive insurance, collision, liability, accident benefits, loss of use.

Business Interruption Insurance: Covers fixed expenses that would continue if, for example, a fire shuts down the business.

Key Person Insurance: Covers the loss of key people in your business through death or prolonged disability that can result in reduced profitability.

Buy-Sell Insurance: A life insurance policy for each company owner's share of the business. If one of the owners dies, a cash settlement is received by his/her estate/family in exchange for his/her business interests.

Business Loan Insurance: Offered through lenders, who receive insurance proceeds to retire company loan principal after the death of the business owner.

Group Insurance: Tailored to provide a combination of life, health, dental, and disability insurance for the benefit of business employees and their families.

Credit Insurance: Protects businesses from unexpected bad debts.

Surety Bonds: Insure against failure of other firms to complete contractual obligations. Frequently used in the construction industry.

PROJECT MANAGEMENT

According to the Project Management Institute (PMI), Project Management is the application knowledge, skills, tools and techniques to a broad range of like activities in order to meet the requirements of a particular project.

Every business, small, medium or large, will encounter the need to utilize project management techniques. Typical projects could be the development of new products or services, assessing the need for a new capital expenditure, or setting up a new e-commerce web site etc.

The Project Management Body of Knowledge – PMBOK recognises 5 basic steps in completing a typical project-management assignment.

Initiating – defining the project planning framework (project charter), and developing a statement of work, requirements and scope definition (what is included and excluded). The major deliverables, milestones and responsibilities will also need to be assessed.

Planning – refining the work breakdown, estimating, assembling the project team and scheduling.

Executing – will need to consider risk management, issue management (including escalation processes) and progress reporting.

Controlling – addressing what needs to be done to keep the project on track to achieve a successful completion.

Closing – report delivery considerations, re-allocation of team members, knowledge management initiatives (to retain and learn from the project undertaken)[4]

LEGAL ISSUES

Which legal structure should you adopt? Here are three basic options:

1. Sole proprietorship
2. Partnership
3. Corporation

1. SOLE PROPRIETORSHIP

Key features:

> ➤ You own the business outright and your business income is treated as personal income.

Advantages:

> ➤ Business losses can be offset against your personal taxable income.
>
> ➤ Lower costs of set-up and operation.
>
> ➤ Less regulation and reporting requirements.

Disadvantages:

> ➤ Limited access to capital.
>
> ➤ You are *personally liable* for all business obligations and any related litigation.
>
> ➤ Some government programs are only available to incorporated entities.

2. PARTNERSHIPS

Key features:

> ➤ Each partner shares in profits/losses based on their percentage interest in the business.
>
> ➤ The partners' responsibilities and obligations are normally defined in a written partnership agreement.

Advantages:

> ➤ Workload and capital requirements are shared.
>
> ➤ New partners can be added, thereby providing more flexibility.
>
> ➤ Partners provide different skill sets, mutual support, and more sources of capital.
>
> ➤ Partners are taxed individually.

Disadvantages:

> ➤ Unlimited liability for partnership debts.

> ➤ Business and personal assets are at risk for any financial losses suffered.

> ➤ One partner can potentially make decisions that bind all others.

> ➤ Dissolution can be difficult and time consuming.

Note: There are limited liability partnerships (LLPs) that limit the amount of personal liability. These are generally used in professional service organizations.

3. CORPORATIONS

Key features:

> ➤ A separate legal entity granted authority by either federal or provincial law.

> ➤ Legally separate from the owners (shareholders).

Advantages:

> ➤ Greater access to sources of capital via share issues (equity) and security agreements (debt).

> ➤ Expanded estate planning benefits.

> ➤ Shareholders are not personally responsible for corporations' debts (unless personal guarantees have been signed).

> ➤ Enhanced image via corporate profile.

> ➤ Internal incentives available to employees (i.e. stock options).

Disadvantages:

> ➤ Higher start-up costs and a more complex regulatory environment.

> ➤ Potentially fewer tax write-offs at commencement of business operations.

Engaging an experienced and skilled commercial lawyer is an essential element to the operations planning process especially before any significant business commitments or decisions are made.

Your commercial lawyer can assist in the following areas:

> Business incorporation and partnership agreement structuring.

> Setting up and negotiating commercial property leases.

> Protecting intellectual property.

> Reviewing franchise agreements.

> Resolving employment issues (terminations, severance agreements).

> Initiating overdue receivable collections.

> Drafting buy/sell agreements between shareholders.

> Structuring legal contracts (joint ventures co-ownership agreements, licensing agreements, etc.).

> Acquisition agreements (buying/selling assets or shares) along with the necessary due diligence.

INFORMATION TECHNOLOGY CONSIDERATIONS

The impact of information or digital technology on company operations is a huge and rapidly evolving topic. In this section we provide:

> A brief summary of computer technology applications that impact company operations.

> An overview of e-commerce opportunities and strategies.

> A new section on Web site assessment.

COMPUTER TECHNOLOGY APPLICATIONS

Computer technology is widely used to track financial, marketing and operational activities.

> Small manufacturers today make extensive use of CAD (Computer Assisted Design) and CAM (Computer Assisted Manufacturing).

> Local Area Networks (LAN) have dramatically improved office automation.

> Customized software is now extensively used for tasks such as payroll, inventory management, billing, customer relationship management and accounting.

➤ Productivity software (word processing, spreadsheet, database management) has generated significant cost savings.

➤ Significant improvements in office technology have taken place through e-mail, voicemail, fax machines, and video conferencing.

➤ Business presentations have been enhanced via multimedia technology that integrates text, audio, graphics, and video.

E-COMMERCE OPPORTUNITIES

Some of the opportunities and issues arising from the rapidly growing world of e-commerce include:

A. Business to Consumer Transactions (B2C)

➤ Emarketer, Inc. forecasts annual US consumer spending via B2C transactions to top US$109 billion in 2004.[5] Despite the post dot.com upheaval, growth in this market has continued steadily, partially in response to increased use of broadband Internet access around the world.

➤ Credit card transactions are a key element of the B2C world. Appropriate security and technology standards are crucial and, while generally secure, are continually being refined.

B. Business-to-Business Transactions (B2B)

➤ Recent research estimates U.S. B2B revenues for 2003 to top $634 billion.[6] These expenditures have grown dramatically over recent years, easily surpassing the historical growth rates observed in the B2C sector. Why? The reason is simple. There are far more separate transactions involving buyers and sellers in the business world. There are two types of B2B companies:

1. Vertical companies: These firms create markets within certain industries (e.g., steel, life sciences, chemicals), thereby allowing companies within the given industry (vertical) to electronically communicate and transact with potential suppliers and customers.

2. Horizontal companies: These companies serve the *same needs* across different industries. *For example:*

   Raw goods procurement – Commerce One and Ariba

   Finished goods shipment -Fedex and UPS

Benefits derived from engaging in B2B e-commerce include:

> Reduced purchasing costs.

> Increased market efficiency with price quotes quickly available from numerous suppliers.

> Increased market intelligence, which provides greater understanding of demand levels in any given market.

> Decreased inventory levels that arise from enhanced 'just in time' processes.

> Increased capacity utilization with excess inventory being turned over via selective online auctions.

WEB SITE ASSESSMENT

The majority of business owners now have a web site that describes their business opportunities and operations. In terms of web site quality and access, they will vary from low-cost 'post-card' offerings to highly professional, well-conceived portals.

We are pleased to present a useful web site evaluation matrix, which is based upon five key indicators, derived from a model developed by Rick Doran.[7] Each indicator will have a 20% weighting with appropriate scores accorded.

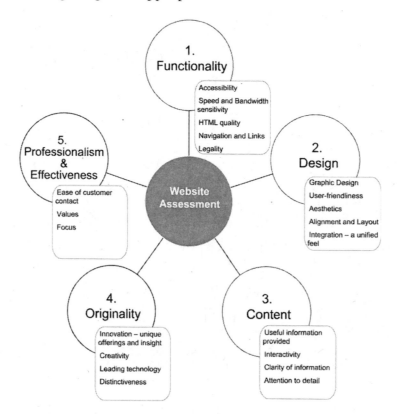

The Operations Review Summary

Stage 1	Stage 2	Stage 3	Stage 4	Stage 5	Stage 6
Process Management	Facilities Management	Inventory Management	Total Quality Management	Risk Management	Project Management

Process Management
- Type of Production
- Link to Marketing Strategy
- Equipment & Technology

Facilities Management
- Location of Physical Facilities
- Home Offices
- Home Shoring
- Incubators
- Lease or Buy

Inventory Management
- ABC method
- Just-in-time inventory system
- Economic Order Quantity

Total Quality Management
- TQM Techniques: Six Sigma
- Define
- Measure
- Analyze
- Improve
- Control

Risk Management
- Types of Business Risks
- Types of Business Insurance

Project Management
- Initiating
- Planning
- Executing
- Controlling
- Closing

USEFUL WEB SITES

www.bettermanagement.com	Insights re business process management
www.ibcpub.com	Logistics Business magazine
www.ifma.org	International facilities management association
www.effectiveinventory.com	Inventory management resources
www.irmi.com	International Risk Management Institute
www.isixsigma.com	Comprehensive Six Sigma resources
www.pmi.com	Project Management Institute web site
www.itaa.org	Information Technology Association of America

Notes from text.

1. http://money.guardian.co.uk/work/story/

2. Jack Welsh – 'Winning' – Harper Business 2005

3. http://www.isixsigma.com/dictionary/DMAIC-57.htm

4. http://www.pmi.org

5. US B2C E-Commerce Tops $90B This Year, April 29, 2003.
   http://www.gcis.ca/n-aa/cdne-500-may-01-2003.html

6. Business Market: The Growth of B2B Market, 2003.
   http://ecommerce.insightin.com/market_research/business_market.html

7. Special thanks to Rick Doran, World Best Websites, www.worldbest.com and Sheila Carruthers-Forget who, in completing her MBA major consulting project, brought this model to our attention.

CHAPTER 6
HUMAN RESOURCES MANAGEMENT

OVERVIEW

In this section, we review the human resource function and examine key characteristics of leadership. Many companies, especially smaller, early stage tend to minimize the importance of this functional area. Human resources is a key contributor to an organization's health and has a strong influence on a company's competitive position in the marketplace.

Hiring and retaining motivated employees, who either support or interface directly with your clients, is a critical success factor.

1. THE HUMAN RESOURCE (HR) FUNCTION

Key Areas:

- ➤ Recruitment and hiring.
- ➤ Training and development.
- ➤ Compensation, performance and incentives.
- ➤ Planning (short and long term).

RECRUITMENT AND HIRING

Issues to consider:

- ➤ The critical importance in 'hiring right' ("Hire for attitude, train for skill")
- ➤ The need to demonstrate to new employees their ability to progress to positions of greater responsibility.

Sources of new employees:

- ➤ Employee referrals
- ➤ Employment agencies
- ➤ Newspaper advertisements
- ➤ Educational institutions (Internships, Co-op Programs, Career Fairs)
- ➤ Competitors

Selection and evaluation of new employees. Some issues to consider:

- ➤ Pro-forma job application forms.
- ➤ A formalized interview process.
- ➤ References (extensive due diligence is required).
- ➤ Determine who has the responsibility for hiring. Does this tie in with reporting relationships?

Retaining good existing employees is a key strategy that requires the establishment of appropriate performance-based evaluation systems and a culture that promotes workplace quality, pride and achievement.

TRAINING AND DEVELOPMENT

Issues to consider:

- ➤ Ineffective training programs can lead to trial and error learning.
- ➤ Orientation of new employees should include an explanation of specific job duties, performance expectations and evaluation processes.
- ➤ Developing 'technology workers' for progression into marketing, sales and project management positions in the knowledge sector involves retraining and the creation of new career paths. This type of retraining is best accomplished by attending practical education programs externally or having them delivered in-house by training consultants.

COMPENSATION, PERFORMANCE AND INCENTIVES

- Employee incentives can be both financial and non-financial.

- Financial compensation must be in line with competitors and should be monitored and reviewed on a regular basis.

- Performance based compensation systems (profit-sharing plans) need to be carefully designed and tied to the key success factors of the organization. This is best accomplished by using external HR specialists, although the cost of this service may be a deterrent to smaller companies.

- Comprehensive benefit packages need to be developed (vacation, medical and dental and life and disability insurance plans).

- Goal setting should be established on an annual basis and linked to a formal performance evaluation process (informally every quarter, formally every year).

This goal-setting process should include:

- Job objectives/responsibilities.

- Performance criteria to be used in annual review.

- exceeded/achieved/ did not achieve plan.

- Performance assessment should include both qualitative and quantitative factors. Criteria and goals should be SMART:

  - **S**pecific
  - **M**easurable
  - **A**chievable
  - **R**elevant
  - **T**ime framed

- Personal development needs (training, seminars, etc.).

- It is important to foster an innovation culture, where employees put forward proposals that have the potential to improve products, services, and processes.

- Employee Equity Incentive Plans

- Employees often have the opportunity to participate in a company's financial growth by way of various equity incentive plans. These include:

    - Group RRSP plans
    - Stock purchase plans
    - Profit sharing
    - Stock options

- Stock options have attained popularity due to the dramatic increase in technology valuations of the past few years.

- Such options provide the right to purchase company common shares at a stated price during a specific period of time. Usually, options are granted with an exercise price equal to the fair market value of the stock at date of grant or hire. If the stock price rises above the exercise price, the option allows the employee to purchase the stock at a lower (exercise) price.

- Vesting periods are the periods of time during which the options are held by the employee but cannot be triggered. There is usually a minimum one year waiting period often followed by 'stepped' vesting periods over the next three to four years.

- Liquidity issues: While there is a potential financial gain to the employee (derived when the stock exercise price is less than the current market value), liquidity (the ability to sell the stock) remains a key consideration, especially if *private* company shares have been vested.

- Such incentive programs have the indirect benefit of locking in (or handcuffing) key employees thereby reducing the risk of their departure to competitors. Clear ground rules need to be established as to the stock disposition process when the employee departs (especially if to a competitor).

HUMAN RESOURCES PLANNING

Short and mid term planning involves the assessment of work force requirements to handle pressing operational tasks. Longer term (strategic) planning involves a forward looking analysis of HR needs to meet the company's growth requirements. Both processes involve:

- Managing growth or market contraction issues.

- Anticipating product or service migrations.

- Assessing the type of employees required.

- Establishing future compensation, training and staff development initiatives.

2. LEADERSHIP

In our view, key leadership skills include setting and communicating strategic vision, marshalling adequate resources, establishing the right organizational structure and acting with integrity.

The following leadership issues and requirements need to be considered in managing a small- or medium-sized business:

ORGANIZATIONAL STRUCTURE

Smaller companies experience continuous organizational and management challenges as they grow. Many of these business owners are generalists and often lack, or cannot afford qualified professional staff.

The stages in the organizational life of a typical small business can be summarized as follows:

> *Level One:* is a one-person operation that does everything.

> *Level Two:* The owner becomes a player/coach and participates extensively in all facets of the business.

> *Level Three:* The owner has hired an intervening layer of management (typically sales and production managers).

> *Level Four:* The management functions are more formalized with more control processes put into place.

Figure 6-1 (next page) illustrates a simple functional organization chart that could be applied to Level Two or Three businesses. The earlier the growth stage, the more likely one person will assume *more than one* functional role.

SKILLS DEVELOPMENT

Developing the following leadership skills will result in a more proactive and effective management team:

> *Listening skills:* Active listening involves looking at issues from others' perspectives and also understanding and learning from them.

> *MBWA* (Management By Walking Around): Communicating with and listening to employees at all levels of the company.

Figure 6-1

A Functional Organizational Chart

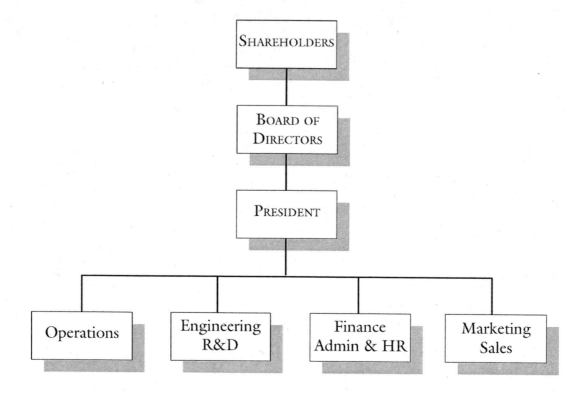

> *Mentoring:* Developing employees for future growth through constructive feedback and teaching.

> *Empowerment:* Strengthening employee beliefs in their own effectiveness. This can be accomplished by ensuring that authority and decision making are progressively pushed to lower and lower levels. Employees are encouraged to embark on reasonable initiatives without fear of retribution.

> *Motivation:* Two concepts that are sometimes considered:

1) '360 degree feedback'.

The process is also known as 'full-circle-feedback' and involves gathering observations about performance from supervisors, peers, subordinates and, sometimes, customers and then linking this feedback to the employee's own self-evaluation.

The intent is to obtain as much frank feedback from as many perspectives as possible.

Potential benefits include:

♦ Team development – individual members will know who is working effectively.

♦ Improved client service – if external clients are asked to participate.

♦ Useful insights gained as to overall training needs.

Concerns with this type of review system include:

♦ Anonymous reviews from staff or colleagues may use the system to settle old scores.

♦ The process can be extremely time-consuming with extensive data collection, evaluation and dissemination required.

♦ The process tends to focus on negatives and problems.

♦ The 'raters' often receive insufficient training.

2) **Open book management**

♦ All employees receive *relevant* information about company's financial performance and condition. This is often tied to profit sharing and/or stock ownership plans.

♦ This process also helps employees see the necessity for change, which is invariably driven by financial realities.

♦ Builds trust so everyone can see what is going on and where the company is headed.

♦ A major concern with this process is the extent to which employees have full access to company financial statements, which often contain confidential information.

TEAMS & TEAMWORK

Within many organizations, employees are teaming up and partnering to solve complex issues under tight time constraints.

TRENDS AND OBSERVATIONS

➤ Teams are now replacing the 'boss-employee' coupling of the past.

➤ Teams today are being formed to maximize competitive advantage and will often consist of members from various countries around the world, operating in a virtual fashion.

> Teams can be functional (i.e., sales teams organized by geography) or cross functional (i.e. engineers and sales people involved in the launch of a new product).

> Effective team performance often takes time to achieve. Utilizing the team's 'collective intelligence' can be a challenge should trust or agenda issues surface.

> Teams fail when their team members are more concerned with individual agendas versus the common goals of the group.

MANAGEMENT CAPABILITIES

Many owners and managers of growing companies 'do not know what they don't know'.

We have prepared the following 'prescriptions' for effective management and leadership. These will allow the reader to assess his or her own capabilities:

> Have you been able to identify your company's key success factors? Those attributes that allow you to successfully compete within your respective industry sector. Can you describe them in a succinct fashion?

> Have you established close and trusting relationships with your key stakeholders? (Employees, customers, suppliers, shareholders, investors etc).

> Are you able to perform a meaningful stakeholder analysis where they can be 'mapped' on the basis of power and interest?

> Is a high standard of ethics and integrity maintained? Do your people know what you stand for?

> Do you possess strong functional management skills in the finance, marketing, operations, HR, technology, and strategic planning areas?

> Assess your level of competence. Someone once said that 'in calm waters, every ship has a good captain'. Being competent, especially from a managerial perspective, involves a complete understanding of your business.

> Are you working *in* the business (head down in the trenches) or are you working *on* the business (assuming a more strategic perspective)?

> Do you give credit where credit is due? Selflessness is an important quality.

> Have you been able to create an understandable and compelling vision for the company – which has an organizational structure that is appropriate for your competitive environment?

> Has the vision and strategic direction been clearly communicated?

➤ Are you able to instill and inspire confidence among your employees to take on challenging tasks and assignments?

➤ Do you encourage risk and invite dissent from your people? At the same time, have they cultivated a sense of urgency and awareness that they need to contribute more than they cost?

➤ Do you emphasize flexibility and the development of skill-sets that allows employees to work across departmental boundaries?

➤ Are you maintaining a broad perspective by asking:

 ♦ What if...? Why do we do this...? What will it take...?

➤ How would you answer these two key questions:

 ♦ What is keeping you awake at night?

 ♦ Where do you see your company in three years time?

A Note on Appreciative Inquiry

Appreciative inquiry (AI) is an organizational development process that was originated by Dr. David L. Cooperrider.

In essence, the methodology is about seeing the glass to be 'half full' as opposed to being 'half-empty' – in other words paying special attention to 'the best of the past and present in order to ignite the collective imagination of what might be'.

In many organizations, there is an unrelenting focus on problem-solving but very little discussion on what has been and is working well.

The AI approach is a useful tool to use as part of the strategic planning process and is a great way for a company owner to hone his/her leadership skills. In such a team based planning session, there would be a review of the organization's capabilities and assets along with focus on what's right.

Such a team experience would be a very transformative process as they uncover and discuss stories about their past successes and peak work experiences.

The outcome is the validation of team members' capabilities, thereby building confidence and the ability to innovate.[1]

Mentoring resources

Running an organization, large, medium or small, can be incredibly lonely with often-important decisions made based upon 'gut feel' without recourse to any objective resources that could provide a more balanced assessment of the situation.

We provide information on three potential useful resources 'that could make the journey less lonely'

1) BOARDS OF DIRECTORS

The benefits derived from establishing an effective Board of Directors include:

> ➢ A competent and active Board of Directors is critical to the capital raising process and company credibility. Board members will often be appointed by early stage investors in the company.

> ➢ The Board ensures that management has developed and implemented a realistic business and strategic plan.

> ➢ Independence and objectivity is provided by outside directors versus using family members, paid professionals or senior management.

> ➢ Carefully selected Board members can provide valuable expertise and contacts that will assist the company's growth.

Some Alternatives:

> ➢ An increased focus on a director's legal responsibilities and liability sometimes makes it difficult to attract talented Board members. A Board of Advisors (or Advisory Board) can be set up, consisting of a similar group of independent and qualified individuals.

Note: A key difference is that the actions of the members are only advisory with the result their personal liability will be reduced. However, appointees should carefully review the terms of their engagement with their corporate lawyer.

> ➢ For start-up companies, the development of an informal mentor network can be a time saving and cost-effective strategy. Mentors can often be accessed through local Chamber of Commerce and technology associations. Retired or semi-retired legal, accounting, commercial banking, consulting professionals or industry specific executives/managers can be an excellent source of informal guidance and feedback.

2) THE EXECUTIVE COMMITTEE (TEC)

TEC was founded by group of non-competing business leaders in 1957 and has since grown to become a global organization with more than 11,000 executive members in 15 countries.

The TEC model includes the sharing of best practices, ongoing professional development and the ability to seek confidential help in critical situations. Each TEC chapter meets for a full day each month with up to 15 members who will be CEOs from non-competing industries. In essence, each participant gains the benefit of a 'collegial board of directors' and receives direct, honest feedback from his/her peers on a monthly basis.

Each chapter is run by a professionally trained TEC Chair who, not only facilitates each monthly meeting but also provides one-to-one coaching to each individual members.[2]

3). THE INTERNATIONAL COACHING FEDERATION (ICF)

There has been a tremendous increase in the demand for executive coaching as leaders of organizations and companies realize that some form of external, objective support is required to guide them on the journey.

The International Coaching Federation (ICF) is the largest nonprofit professional coaching Association worldwide with over 132 chapters in 34 countries. Their mandate is to build, support and preserve the integrity of the coaching profession.

Professional ICF coaches undergo a rigorous certification process and are bound by a code of ethics. Coaches work in partnership with their clients and are trained to listen, observe and customize their coaching approach to the individual's needs.[3]

A key element to their approach is a 'nondirective' coaching. The client chooses the focus of conversation, while the coach listens, contributes observations and open-ended questions. Through this coaching process, 'self developed clarity' leads to the crafting of the most appropriate and effective action plans.

USEFUL WEB SITES

www.inc.com	Inc. web site – excellent HR information section
www.coachfederation.org	International Coaching Federation website
www.360-degreefeedback.com	360° feedback information and software
www.successfactors.com	Workforce performance management
www.talentsmart.com	Leadership white papers
www.teconline.com	The Executive Committee (TEC) website

Notes from text.

1. http://www.appreciative-inquiry.org
2. http://www.teconline.com
3. www.coachfederation.org

CHAPTER 7
THE TECHNOLOGY ASSESSMENT

OVERVIEW

A significant number of companies are now operating in the High Tech or Knowledge- Based Industry (KBI) sector. Given the increasing importance of technology issues, a technology assessment is included as a final element of the Internal Size-Up.

Even if your company is not directly operating as a technology company, it is highly likely that either your suppliers or clients (or both) are technology companies. This assessment process provides some insights as to their potential and their challenges; in essence, how long they might be around.

The assessment consists of the following areas:

1. Technology description

2. Products/services and processes

3. Intellectual property issues

4. Markets

5. Potential risk factors

6. New Technology evaluation

Investment and pay back considerations would normally be incorporated into such an assessment process; however, these issues are dealt with in more detail in Chapter Nine.

We wish to thank Denzil Doyle for his assistance with certain sections of this chapter – his excellent book *Making Technology Happen* has been used as a valuable reference point, with suitable permission granted.

1. TECHNOLOGY DESCRIPTION

Consider:

➢ What is the technology and the opportunity? Can this be summarized to a stranger in an elevator within 30 seconds? If not, develop a 30-second message.

➢ What is the development stage? Technology push or Market pull?

Technology 'pushers': Are the developers and inventors who enthusiastically push and promote their new technology although their products and markets have yet to be clearly identified. Once the markets are identified, they attempt to push even harder!

Market 'pullers': Are completely familiar with a given market and have identified the need for a product. They then set out to pull their product through a technology development process.

These relationships are illustrated in Figure 7-1 (below). To quote Denzil Doyle (Making Technology Happen) – Ask the following simple question, "What is the product and how much of it can be sold?"

Figure 7-1

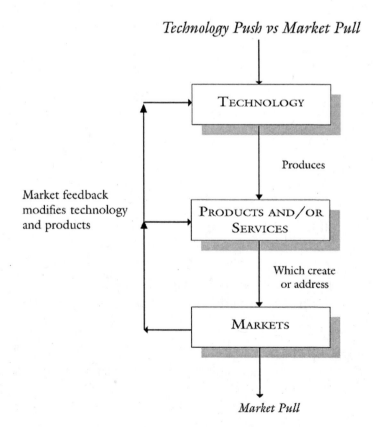

Technology Push vs Market Pull

2. PRODUCTS/SERVICES AND PROCESSES

Consider:

> What is the purpose of the product or service?

> Does it meet potential customer needs?

> What are the unique features? Cost, design, simplicity?

> What is the estimated technological life?

> At what stage is the product on the innovation chain?

  1. Idea: Tend to be easy to generate and easy to kill.
  2. R&D: Technical stage or market stage?
  3. Development: Engineering prototype, pilot run, client evaluations.
  4. Production: Product testing and refinements.
  5. Market development: Beta testing, setting up distribution channels.

> What type of production processes will be employed?

  ♦ capital intensive
  ♦ labor intensive
  ♦ material intensive

> Is there a product migration (follow-on) product strategy?

Consider:

> One-product technology companies are often doomed to failure.

> 'Follow on' products will ideally consist of two new additions to the product family.

  i) one with a lower price and lower functionality.
  ii) one with a higher price and higher functionality.

> An effective product migration strategy will lead to timely product introductions so that new products generate revenues at the same time as old ones are reaching maturity or starting to decline.

3. INTELLECTUAL PROPERTY ISSUES

Safeguarding intellectual property is a complex yet essential task for technology companies. The status of a company's intellectual property (IP) is a key area of focus and due diligence by potential investors.

The following brief review highlights the various types of IP protection:

A) PATENTS

> A patent does **not** grant individual exclusive rights to an invention in Canada. The patent is granted to the inventor who is first to file an application. In the U.S it can be granted to the first to invent rather than the first to file.

> The inventor is granted a 'negative right' under the law and is able to exclude others from using and making the invention. This right is granted in exchange for making the patent information known to the public.

> In Canada, present patent legislation presently grants the owner the legal right to exclude others from using the patentable invention for 20 years from the date of filing. Patents are ***not*** renewable once the 20-year time period has elapsed.

KEY QUESTIONS TO ASK PRIOR TO IMPLEMENTING A PATENT STRATEGY

> Is there an existing or potential market for the invention?

> What are the costs to manufacture and market the invention?

> Is funding in place to commercially exploit the invention?

REQUIREMENTS FOR A PATENT

i) **Utility:** Does the device or process have a practical benefit that meets customer needs?

ii) **Novelty:** The invention has to be new.

   Note: If the invention has been publicly disclosed, developed, or sold more than one year prior to a Canadian or USA patent application, the patent application will be denied.

iii) **Inventive ingenuity:** The invention must be 'non obvious'. It must be an improvement or development that is not obvious to anyone possessing average skill in the technology field.

THE REGISTRATION PROCESS

➤ Preliminary search: Usually carried out in the Canadian and USA patent offices. A broader and more comprehensive 'infringement search' can also be completed to see if the invention infringes another patent.

➤ Preparation and filing of the application: Use an experienced patent lawyer or agent to guide you through this complex process.

➤ The registration process involves drafting an application that:

♦ Clearly distinguishes your invention from previous ones.

♦ Defines specific claims, which establish the scope and quality of the patent.

ACCEPTANCE OR REJECTION

If accepted, the patent holder has the legal right to exclude others from using, making, or selling the invention at the date of approval. It should be noted that up to three years could often elapse from the initial application, due to the considerable volume of patent applications currently being filed.

B) PATENT PENDING

This status can be placed or affixed to a device or process after filing the patent application and prior to registration. It has no legal effect. It serves to warn others and, in some ways, can offer more protection than if the patent had been formally accepted.

The invention details are not revealed by the government to outsiders for the period of time during the application process.

Potential competitors may be deterred from copying for fear of infringing on the forthcoming patent.

C) TRADE SECRETS

A **trade secret** is a process, design or compilation of specific technical data that is used by a company to ensure its competitive advantage over others who do not have access to such closely guarded information.

Trade secrets have no protection under the law (as opposed to patents or trademarks) – the most significant difference between them is that the trade secret is protected without having to disclose its closely held information.

A key tool in maintaining the trade secret is often the requirement for a Non-Disclosure Agreement (NDA) to be completed by key employees. Such agreements will call for employees to confirm that they will not reveal the employer's proprietary information and the requirement that they waive any intellectual property rights associated with the project

A classic example of a trade secret is Coca Cola – the company has no patents for its formula, choosing instead to keep information closely guarded.

One drawback of a trade secret is that the product in question may be subject to reverse engineering.

d) Trademarks

> Trademarks are any name, symbol, or expression which an individual or organization uses to distinguish its products or services.

> In Canada, the first person to use a trademark is entitled to register the mark and obtain exclusive rights. The trademark is registered for 15 years from the date of registration and is renewable.

Benefits in registering trademarks include:

> Alerts others of its existence.

> Provides nation-wide protection.

> Allows a holder to commence trademark infringement proceedings.

e) Copyright

> Copyright protection provides artists/authors with the sole right to transmit, reproduce, sell and distribute their work or to permit someone else to do so.

> Protection lasts for the author's lifetime plus 50 years after the author's death.

> In Canada, copyright is automatically conferred upon the creator of an original work without registration.

> Registration is voluntary but advisable. This step provides the owner with a basis to commence a copyright infringement action if required.

F) INDUSTRIAL DESIGN

- Can be registered for a single term of 10 years.

- Prevents other firms from directly copying a design.

- Protects the design of a functional device or object.

- Additional intellectual property rights are available within specific industries.

G) CONFIDENTIALITY AND EMPLOYMENT AGREEMENTS

- Essential for an organization to protect its technology by ensuring that outsiders and key employees have signed and are legally bound by written agreements. A Non Disclosure Agreement (NDA) would fall under this category.

H) ACCESS RESTRICTIONS

- To production, laboratory research facilities, data storage areas. This process should also include a disaster recovery plan (fire, flood, earthquake).

COMPLETION OF AN INTELLECTUAL PROPERTY PLAN

Steps:

- Complete an Intellectual Property (IP) audit to identify and inventory IP assets. The process includes a review of records management, confidentiality practices, and contracts administration.

- Analyze IP strengths and weaknesses. Decide what technologies to develop and ask "is leadership in these technologies affordable?" Can you "license-in" some outside technological processes?

- Ensure inventors are product driven. Company engineers should file patents as an ongoing and integral part of product development. They should also complete patent infringement searches as part of the pre-design process.

- Develop a budget for patent costs.

- Initiate an IP training program for key employees.

4. Markets

Technology companies often attempt to market their products or services based on technical abilities rather than satisfying customer needs.

Consider the following questions:

> ➤ Have you assessed your market potential in relation to total market size?

> ➤ What is your expected market penetration and market share?

> ➤ Assess replacement versus incremental markets?

> ➤ Replacement sales are those that involve the replacement of existing units. Buyers are normally influenced by price or increased quality.

> ➤ Incremental sales are those made to 'early adopters and visionaries' who are influenced by product functionality and newness versus price.

> ➤ Understand your distribution channels. Are distribution agreements mutually advantageous?

> ➤ Has a detailed marketing plan been completed, identifying target market segments?

> ➤ Licensing opportunities.
> If a technology process is initiated and is not suitable for development into a discrete product or service, can it be licensed for use in other operations?

Some benefits of licensing:

> ➤ Licensees (receiving the technology) have existing products or facilities and are able to acquire the technology more cheaply and quickly than by completing their own R&D process.

> ➤ The licenser is able to exploit its technology in secondary markets without large marketing and production expenditures.

> ➤ Licensing is an effective way to test and develop offshore markets.

> ➤ Licensees are unlikely to become future competitors.

5. POTENTIAL RISK FACTORS

SOME KEY QUESTIONS TO CONSIDER

- Is there a threat of emerging new competitors and/or superior technology?

- How short are your product life-cycles with resulting obsolescence issues?

- What is the relationship between the stage of technology development and cash flow generation?

- The negative cash flow experienced during the earlier stages of product development, along with unexpected expenditure surprises, can lead to feelings of despair in the 'valley of uncertainty'. As operations ramp up to meet market demand, cash flow shortfalls begin to diminish, leading to increasing optimism.

- How mobile are key employees and management? Is there potential to lose intellectual property 'walking out of the door'? Can this be counteracted by stock option incentives (handcuffs) and/or non-compete agreements?

- Are there growth-related risks? What would be the impact be on

  - ◆ Production?
  - ◆ Human Resources?
  - ◆ Finances?
  - ◆ Marketing and sales?

- Is there a dependence on a limited number of customers?

- Is there a dependence on a limited number of suppliers? Are there alternative sources of supply or does the potential to outsource exist?

- How strong are your proprietary rights? Is there potential for infringement lawsuits?

- Is there a currency or foreign receivable risk? Can these be hedged or insured by the Export Development Corporation (EDC)?

- Do you have the financial resources to cover ongoing R&D costs that are necessary for product enhancements and the development of new generation technologies?

- Do you have the ability to raise additional capital via committed investors with deep pockets?

Figure 7-2 (below) illustrates the often-painful process in completing product development while experiencing severe cash flow constraints.

Figure 7-2

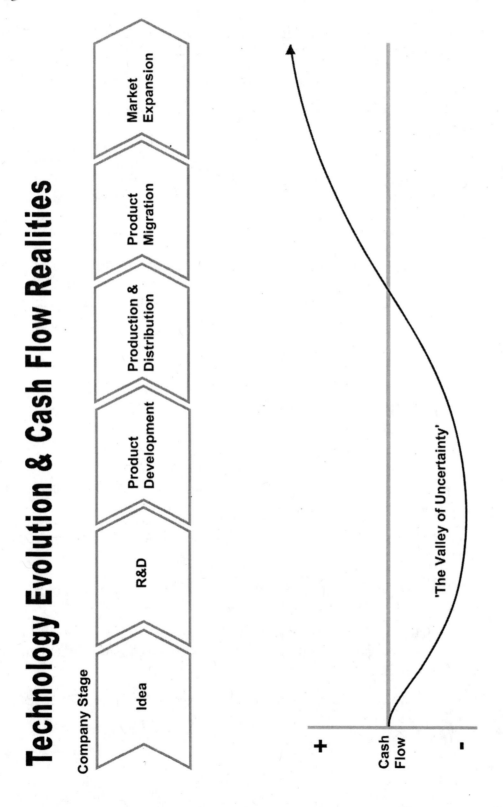

Technology Evolution & Cash Flow Realities

Company Stage: Idea | R&D | Product Development | Production & Distribution | Product Migration | Market Expansion

Cash Flow: + / −

'The Valley of Uncertainty'

6. NEW TECHNOLOGY ASSESSMENTS

This concluding section covers an eight-step process that can be used to determine the potential for a new technology to succeed.[1]

Often a company will consider acquiring or developing a new technology in order to boost their growth strategies – developing a new product for new markets can be a highly risky undertaking, as you will see in our case study – Marston Control Devices, where a new robotic medical device technology application is being launched.

If you were a professional advisor to John Marston, here are some key questions that you would ask:

1) *What are the strategic benefits of this new technology to the organization?*

When obtaining information about strategic benefits, don't limit the list to only those promoted or provided by the technology developers. The experience gained by others is also an important way to identify additional strategic benefits.

For business purposes, strategic benefits are a primary consideration; other factors are secondary. If there are few strategic benefits that a new technology can bring to your organization, there is little reason for an organization to pursue it any further.

2) *What are the key issues that have caused a demand for this new technology?*

This question will separate strategically beneficial, bona fide technologies from those that may be viewed as 'solutions looking for problems'.

If the new technology meets an existing, defined demand, there will be a resulting tangible benefit.

3) *What does this new technology consist of?*

Technologies, described as "new," may be repackaged old technologies, or re-engineered, newer technologies from an unreceptive market. Understanding the differences is key.

Understanding the original technology, and the environment in which it operates, can help place new applications into perspective.

Familiarity with a new technology at an overview level will help you appreciate how the pieces fit together. For example, "Web Services" as a whole can be most confusing, but once it is understood that as a technology, it consists primarily of standards to enable one web-based application to share program functionality with others on either side of the firewall, then much of the mystique is dispelled.

4) *What are the current statistics and trends?*

Statistics and trends provide a contextual background for a new technology. They provide insight into the popularity of a technology, and indicate how established it has become. Inevitably, adoption of an immature technology raises risk-related concerns for most organizations. As a result, it is important to review statistics and trends to gain meaningful insight into the maturity and corresponding stability of the technology.

For volatile and non-volatile technologies, statistics and trends can be of significant value in assessing risk. Statistics and trends are a key indicator of maturity. For the professional advisor, it's important to be aware of which technologies are likely to be of higher risk than others.

5) *Who are the vendors (developers) for this technology?*

Knowing the principal vendors, the nature of the products they supply and understanding the differences between their products is key to attaining a practical, broad-based knowledge of the technology and its functionality.

For example, more and more, vendors now are putting customer case studies on their Web sites to provide useful insight into what customers are doing with their products, while also offering useful leads for follow up.

In higher risk situations, where the vendor is more likely to be a business partner, the vendor and product functionality play a pivotal role in a successful implementation.

6) *Who is using this technology and what can be learned from its use?*

There is no substitute for the real thing – gaining an insight into the implementation of the technology by at least one organization and learning about the experiences encountered.

Such an organization can be selected by going through the vendor or obtaining a referral from others, such as industry associations. In some cases, those interviewed may be quite candid in sharing the experiences they gained in adopting a new technology and, as such, will make an invaluable contribution.

7) *What are the strategic planning issues that need to be considered?*

Essential to the successful implementation of a new technology is careful planning.

Inherent is the need to define strategic objectives and anticipate the kind of risks, pitfalls and problems that may be encountered along the way. Comments made by those interviewed in the past who have implemented new technologies have included such remarks as, "I wish we had spent more time planning."

It is clear that forward-thinking strategic and planning decisions have to be made to ensure the successful implementation of a new technology. Finding out what kind of problems can be anticipated, and being prepared to address them, will help to minimize the possibility of a new technology initiative becoming derailed.

8) *What have other's experiences been in implementing this technology?*

Gaining a cross-section of implementation experiences and feedback from others helps to build on successes, as well as avoiding the possibility of repeating the mistakes made by others. You need to understand that 'success' is still largely a matter of perception – a technological success does not necessarily mean project success.

The media both on and off the Internet are good sources of experiences, bearing in mind that the failures are more likely to make the headlines than quiet successes. In using the media as a source, it is worthwhile noting that it can be used as a stepping stone, insofar as the people quoted will usually be willing to provide further insight when contacted directly.

USEFUL WEB SITES

www.ipmall.fplc.edu/	Intellectual property mall – Franklin Pierce
www.redherring.com	Red Herring – business of technology
www.lawguru.com	Access to legal search engines (I.P issues)
www.inc.com/resources/technology	Inc. guide to business technology

Notes from text.

1. Based upon an article titled *A Logical Approach to Understanding New Technologies* by Jonathan D. Andrews FCA. Abridged with kind permission from the author.

Notes

SECTION 3

THE COMPANY LIFE CYCLE AND RELATED FUNDING INITIATIVES

Business Diagnostics Overview

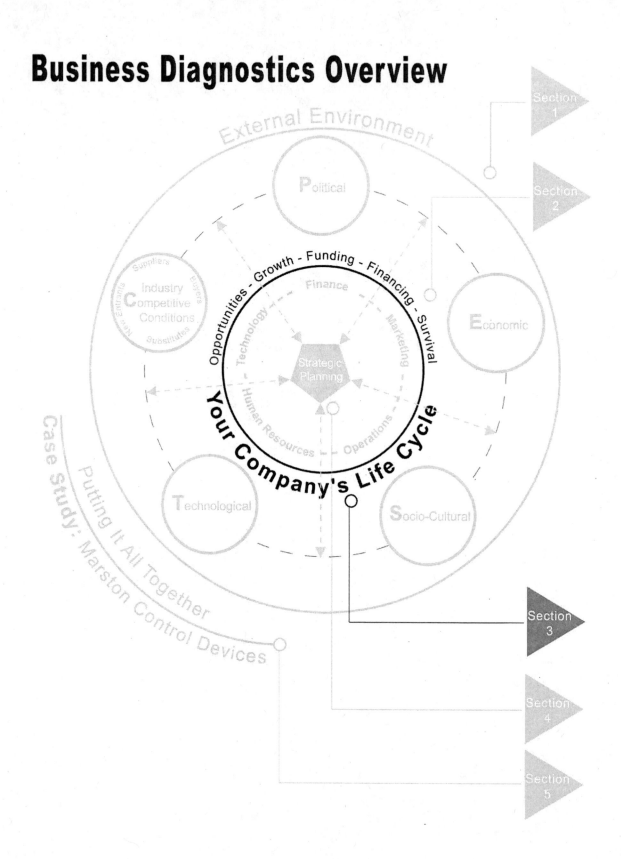

External Environment

Political

Economic

Socio-Cultural

Technological

Suppliers
Buyers
New Entrants
Substitutes
Industry Competitive Conditions

Opportunities - Growth - Funding - Financing - Survival

Finance
Marketing
Operations
Human Resources
Technology

Strategic Planning

Your Company's Life Cycle

Case Study: Marston Control Devices

Putting It All Together

Section 1

Section 2

Section 3

Section 4

Section 5

CHAPTER 8
NEW BUSINESS OPPORTUNITIES AND STRATEGIES

OVERVIEW

This chapter deals with the first stage of evolution that business owners encounter -the new business opportunity.

The following key areas will be reviewed:

1. Self Assessment

2. The Start-up process

3. Buying an existing business

4. Valuation issues

5. Buying a franchise operation

6. Entering a family business

7. Characteristics of successful new business ventures

1. SELF ASSESSMENT

We have developed a two-stage checklist, which will permit an aspiring entrepreneur to critically assess his or her ability to succeed in their new business endeavor.

A. THE PROPOSED BUSINESS VENTURE

Some key questions to consider:

➤ Do you have the necessary experience and knowledge to operate the business?

➤ Do you have any practical experience in sales, marketing, finance, or human resource management?

➤ Will the venture actually be a "job disguised as a business"?

➤ Does the business have the potential to reward you for your time, effort, hard work and sleepless nights?

➤ Will there be future opportunities to expand or diversify the business?

➤ A simple but powerful question – what is the product/service and who will buy it?

➤ How easily could a potential competitor start a similar business?

➤ How much control will suppliers (materials and labor) have?

➤ How many employees are required? What level and types of compensation are necessary?

➤ Do you have an experienced accountant, lawyer, and commercial banker in place?

➤ Who will take over if something happens to you? Do you have a succession plan in place?

B. YOUR PERSONAL RESOURCES AND CHARACTERISTICS

➤ Are you willing to risk your savings in this venture? Does the opportunity involve additional personal debt?

➤ Do you have the commitment of your family? Is spousal or a secondary source of income available to support you?

➤ How long could your family accept a temporary drop in income?

➤ Do you have strong leadership and decision-making skills?

➤ Are you able to set priorities and keep to them?

➤ Do you have a strong work ethic, undeterred by long hours and lost weekends?

➤ Are you able to make carefully rationalized decisions and then stick with them?

➤ Are you in good health and able to maintain high levels of activity?

➤ Do you have access to an informal or formal mentoring network?

2. THE START-UP

Starting a business from scratch is a complex and challenging exercise. The following steps describe the process:

A)   THE OPPORTUNITY

➤ To what extent is there a 'window of opportunity' to exploit your idea, product, or service? What is the potential size of the market? How fast can the market grow?

➤ Will the potential earnings be sufficient to provide an acceptable return on your capital and time? Are the earnings sustainable or will they be subject to peaks and valleys?

➤ Does the proposed product or service meet a tangible and, likely, urgent need? Is there 'pain' in the marketplace that you are able to address?

➤ Could this opportunity lead to additional avenues for market expansion or product diversification?

➤ Will the business generate strong profits and *cash flow generation* – avoiding over dependence on inventories and accounts receivable?

B)   DEFINING THE BUSINESS STRATEGY

➤ Are barriers to entry in place or can they be easily created to deter emerging competition? (Example: the early registration of trademarks or copyrights.)

➤ Have market segments and target clients been identified and researched? What distribution channels are available to access these customers?

➤ *Supplier power:* Are you dependent on a few suppliers who control critical inputs to your proposed product or service?

➤ *Buyer power:* Will buyers (your future clients) expect pricing concessions as you endeavor to launch your product?

➤ Have you completed a Strategic Business Plan or at a minimum, an Enterprise Review Summary (see Chapter 9), to secure satisfactory sources of funding?

C)   RESOURCE EVALUATION

➤ What personnel, capabilities, and relationships are already in place? Which ones are required in the future?

➤ What makes the proposed venture unique? Have the necessary proprietary and value-added attributes been protected?

➤ What are the regulatory and legal requirements associated with running the business?

➤ Are there adequate financial and operational resources available to overcome unexpected obstacles and setbacks?

➤ Do the shareholders have access to personal funds, which could be injected as shareholder loans in the event of an emergency?

➤ There are various ways to *acquire* specific resources for the new venture that not involve significant, upfront, cash expenditures.

> *Consider the following:*
> - ◆ Renting – equipment
> - ◆ Leasing – premises
> - ◆ Borrowing – funds for working capital
> - ◆ Subcontracting – employees

➤ How will the right employees and supporting professionals be selected?

➤ What types of incentives need to be offered to your personnel?

➤ How will the owner's roles and responsibilities be delegated as the company grows?

D)   EXIT STRATEGIES

After running a successful business, the owners need to formulate a suitable *exit* strategy.

Exit strategy options include:

- Sale of company to an outside party or to management/ employees (MBO).

- Acquisition by larger company, which could be a competitor, supplier or client.

- Public offering (IPO).

- Liquidation: Sale of assets, debt repayment, and distribution of proceeds to the owner(s).

3. BUYING A BUSINESS

Use the following four-step checklist when deciding whether to buy an existing business:

A. WHY PURCHASE?

- **Favorable Price**: The company is being purchased at a price below the estimated costs of starting a new business.

- **Proven Track Record**: Uncertainties will be reduced when buying an existing business, which already has a demonstrated track record in place.

- **Established Relationships**: Already in place with clients, suppliers, and work force.

- **Solid Market Profile**: Existing target market segments are understood and developed.

B. WHERE TO LOOK?

The following are some information sources that will assist you in your search process:

- Newspaper and business magazine advertisements

- Trade journals

- Business brokers and commercial realtors

➤ Trustees and Receivers

➤ Local economic development and technology association offices

➤ Professional advisors (accountants, lawyers, commercial bankers)

➤ Internet search engines

C. REASONS FOR SALE?

➤ Lack of succession plans and no apparent heirs.

➤ Owners' retirement or ill health.

➤ Owner has other investments or businesses competing for his or her time.

➤ The business expanded too fast, resulting in depleted cash resources and an inability to attract additional equity capital.

➤ Partnership problems (absence of shareholder agreements)

➤ Lost enthusiasm, reduced commitment, fatigue.

➤ Specific industry sector has reached maturity or is in decline.

➤ Local economy is weak.

➤ Increasing competitive pressures.

➤ Outdated technology infrastructure and systems.

➤ Litigation potential or legal actions in process (buy assets not shares!).

➤ Lease renewal is too expensive.

D. THE EVALUATION PROCESS

The following factors will influence the potential selling price of a business:

➤ *Management:* Assess the quality and performance of existing management.

➤ *Financing:* How much debt is carried by the business (is there pressure from creditors and/or the bank?)

➤ Is a *Vendor take-back* (VTB) available to assist with the funding of the purchase price?

➤ *Quality of assets*

> Accounts receivable – what has been the collection track record?
>
> Inventory – any obsolescence issues?
>
> Fixed assets -estimated current market value and remaining economic life?

➤ *Leases*

> Transferable? Maturity dates? Escalation clauses?

➤ *Intellectual property assets:* Are there patents or trademarks in place?

➤ *Competition:* has a current competitor assessment be completed? Is there a potential for big-box competition?

➤ *Financial history:* Revenue, earnings, cash generation performance?

➤ *Warranties:* How many have been extended? What is their duration? Is there any potential financial exposure?

➤ *Legal commitments:* Are there any contingent liabilities, unsettled lawsuits, or any overdue rent payments?

➤ *Product prices:* Have these been compared to competitor price levels? How does the business gross profit margin compare to industry averages?

4. VALUATION TECHNIQUES – WHAT PRICE DO YOU PAY?

Valuing a business is a complex process and is not an exact science. A brief overview is presented here. It is essential to obtain professional advice (accountant, lawyer and/or chartered business valuator) in structuring a formal purchase agreement for a business.

The following valuation approaches will be considered:

A. Asset valuations

B. Market valuations

C. Cash Flow valuations

D. Earnings valuations

A. Asset-Based Valuation – there are three varieties

1) *Modified book value:*

Determined by adjusting the book value to reflect the difference between the historical cost and current value of the assets.

Adjustments will be made for any surplus appraisal value on land and buildings, while intangible asset values would be heavily discounted.

2) *Replacement value:* Value is based on the cost to replace the firm's assets.

3) *Liquidation value:* Value is based on the funds available if a firm was to liquidate its assets.

A weakness to these approaches is that they all fail to recognize the firm as a 'going concern' that generates sustainable revenue and earnings.

B. Market-Based Valuation

This approach is based on actual market prices of firms that have recently been sold or are trading publicly on a stock exchange.

Calculation:

Price Earnings Ratio = $\dfrac{\text{Market Price}}{\text{After tax earnings}}$

Weaknesses:

♦ Finding appropriate multiple comparables is difficult.

♦ Public company data is not likely appropriate given differences in the scale of business operations.

C. Cash flow Valuations

Involves estimating a company's *future* operating cash flows (EBITDA minus regular capital expenditures) and discounting back to a *present value* using the investors required rate of return.

This rate of return would be computed by starting with a 'risk free' rate of return (present treasury bill rate) *plus* a risk premium usually between 10% and 30% depending on the size of the company and associated risk factors.

Additionally, the opportunity cost of the invested funds (alternate uses) needs to be considered.

D. EARNINGS-BASED VALUATION:

The estimated value of the firm is based on its ability to generate future, sustainable earnings.

Process: Derive an estimate of stabilized earnings by considering:

Historical earnings: Use average earnings for the past five years and adjust for non-recurring revenue or expense items.

Future earnings: Those anticipated under present ownership.

Note: The purchaser may derive a different (higher or lower) future earnings estimate based on efficiencies arising from new management (higher earnings) or restructuring costs (lower earnings) that will have an impact on price negotiations.

A KEY QUESTION — WHAT EARNINGS?

There is considerable debate as to which 'earnings' definition should be used in the earnings valuation calculation.

Three earnings definitions:

1. *Earnings after tax:* i.e., net profit before any allowance for extraordinary items.

2. *EBIT:* Earnings before interest and taxes. Measures the earning power and value of the underlying business without the effects of financing.

3. *EBITDA:* Earnings before interest, taxes, depreciation, and amortization. A more accurate measure of cash flows generated by a business.

For small-to medium- sized businesses, the most realistic valuation technique usually involves EBIT, especially if the financing (interest) effect is not shown.

NEXT STEP: DERIVE A CAPITALIZATION RATE (CAP RATE)

The cap rate can also be presented as a multiple (reciprocal).

Example:

	Cap Rate	Multiple	
Low Risk, Higher Value	20%	5x	100/20
	25%	4x	100/25
Higher Risk, Low Value	33%	3x	100/33

The cap rate selection will be somewhat subjective and is derived from a blend of quantitative and qualitative factors. These include the following:

- ➤ P/E ratios of comparable publicly traded companies.

- ➤ Earnings multiples derived from recent company acquisitions in the same industry.

- ➤ Industry rules of thumb adjusted for a company's size and track record (internal value factors).

Internal value factors:

- ➤ Financial: Relative strength of balance sheet, absence of intangible assets, and availability of working capital resources.

- ➤ Marketing: A broad, diversified client base, allied with significant penetration into a company's market segment. Unique products or services with the opportunity to increase future sales and earnings.

- ➤ Operations: The capacity of plant and equipment to handle future growth. Flexibility and versatility of machinery to produce new and different products.

It is important to consider surplus assets: i.e., those that do not contribute directly to the company operations. For example, permanent term deposits or a securities portfolio would be added to the capitalized value.

Example: Earnings-based valuation

Company XYZ

- ➤ Maintainable future earnings (EBIT) per year $155,000

  - ♦ Have been derived from the past Five years income statements and adjusted for non-recurring revenue and expense items.

- These estimated earnings most likely to be realized in the future under present ownership.

➢ Cap rate/multiple   25% (4x)

- Equivalent to business risk based on review of current industry multiples (if available) and company's internal value factors.
- Will need to meet the purchaser's minimum required rate of return.

➢ Surplus assets – term deposits $45,000

VALUATION

Capitalized earnings	4 x $155,000 =	$620,000
Plus: Surplus assets		$ 45,000
Total estimated value		**$665,000**

The Marston Control Devices Ltd. case study (in Section 5) contains a section on current and projected company valuations, which will allow the reader to further, refine their corporate valuation skills.

OTHER RELATED ISSUES

Goodwill: The difference between the tangible net worth of the company and the actual purchase price.

Example:

Company Book equity	$ 80,000
Purchase price	$140,000
Goodwill	**$ 60,000**

Goodwill is an intangible asset that will appear on the *new company's* financial statements. In essence, this 'purchase premium' relates to a basket of intangibles encompassing copyrights, brand name, supplier connections, lease benefits, and location.

The seller will take the position that these intangible factors contribute to earnings generation and, therefore, should have an ascribed value.

A buyer's reluctance to pay a goodwill premium is often mitigated by negotiating an 'earn out' where the vendor takes back financing approximating the agreed value of goodwill. The buyer then pays back the obligation over a negotiated period of time from ongoing company earnings.

PURCHASE OF ASSETS VERSUS SHARES

➤ *Asset Purchase*

- ♦ The buyer sets up a new corporation and transfers all purchased assets (and property lease, if appropriate) into the new corporation.
- ♦ The buyer will attempt to allocate:
- ♦ a low % purchase price for goodwill (if any) as tax write-offs are not as attractive for goodwill as for fixed assets.
- ♦ a high % purchase price will be allocated to depreciable assets to maximize depreciation deductions in the future.

Note: Assets need to be free and clear of any encumbrances, liens, mortgages and/or security agreements.

➤ *Shares Purchase*

- ♦ The buyer purchases company shares from departing shareholders, and elects his/her own directors and officers.
- ♦ Debt can be assumed with the vendor receiving the difference between the purchase price and outstanding debt.
- ♦ Leases, contracts, and licenses typically transfer with the change of share ownership.
- ♦ Tax losses may be available for the benefit of the buyer.
- ♦ Past liabilities (direct or contingent) stay with the company and could come back to haunt the new owner.

Which is the best option? It depends on the various benefits accruing to the purchaser and vendor.

The vendor generally wants to take the 'share sale' option, benefiting from the $500,000 capital gains deduction available to qualified small business corporations and, at the same time, avoiding any 'recapture' costs associated with an asset sale.

The purchaser usually prefers the 'asset purchase' option in order to take advantage of potential Business Improvement Loan financing for equipment and higher depreciation charges for tax purposes. Also, any unknown problems associated with a share purchase (unattractive contracts and/or employee-related issues) can be avoided.

5. FRANCHISE OPPORTUNITIES

OVERVIEW

A franchise is a special type of partnership where one company (the franchisor) grants the right to sell its products and services to another company or individual (the franchisee).

The most common type of franchise is the *Business Format* franchise. The business format is highly controlled with every aspect of the business having been "blueprinted" by the franchisor. Example – Second Cup, Speedy Muffler, Burger King.

Another type of franchise is *Dealership Relationship* franchises. These are less restrictive and involve a licensing or associate relationship. Example – Home Hardware, Century 21, Auto dealers

Franchises are often viewed as a less risky alternative to business ownership. The following brief assessment is provided:

ADVANTAGES OF FRANCHISING

> Lower risk of business failure due to proven track record throughout the franchise network

> Brand name recognition

> Franchiser support

- ♦ employee selection/training
- ♦ inventory control
- ♦ vendor supplies
- ♦ lease negotiations

> Financial support

- ♦ preferential financing packages often including inventory buyback agreements between the franchisor and the franchisee's bank.
- ♦ flexible payment terms to suppliers or product purchases from parent organization.
- ♦ increased purchasing power.
- ♦ additional franchising opportunities to acquire other nearby locations.

FRANCHISING HAZARDS TO AVOID

> Excessive up-front franchise fees and ongoing royalty fees (based on a fixed percentage of annual sales which vary from 2% to 15%).

> Excessive advertising and promotional fees with a nominal local benefit received.

> Growth restrictions – the franchisee is often restricted to a defined sales territory.

> Encroachment – the franchisor initiates alternate distribution channels (Internet sales, gas station outlets, etc.) that effectively compete with the existing franchisee operation.

> Differing legislative protection between states or provinces

> Mature products or services within saturated markets.

> Preference to insiders where existing franchisees are offered prime locations before first time franchise buyers.

> Restrictions on supply-chain relationships.

> Restrictions on selling out – thereby creating high 'exit barriers'.

KEY QUESTIONS TO ASK A FRANCHISOR

As part of the due diligence process, ask the following questions:

> How long has the franchise been in business?

> How many franchise outlets are currently in operation?

> How many failures have there been over the past five years? What were the reasons for such failures?

> Is there any litigation in process?

> Against the franchisor from outside parties?

> Between the franchisor and franchisees?

> How many new franchises have been sold over the past five years?

> Does the franchisor have the right to buy out franchisees? How would the price be determined?

> How financially sound is the franchise? Are franchisor financial statements and bank references available?

- ➤ Does the franchisor have a borrowing relationship with a bank, if so what are the terms and amounts of facilities?

- ➤ How many franchises are operating in the proposed market area?

- ➤ Who is the competition – local and national?

- ➤ What are the fees (upfront, royalty, advertising)? How do these compare to industry averages?

- ➤ What support is provided?
  - ◆ training
  - ◆ lease negotiation
  - ◆ financing
  - ◆ advertising
  - ◆ supplier discounts

- ➤ Are a number of (recent) franchisee references available? Are you able to make contact with them?

6. FAMILY BUSINESS OPPORTUNITIES

Another route to commencing a new venture is the entry to a family-owned business. This opportunity has its own unique characteristics.

Some issues to consider:

- ➤ A key benefit can be the strength of family relationships that often help overcome serious operational setbacks.

- ➤ The founder will invariably leave a deep impact on the culture of the family firm.

- ➤ Changes in culture often occur as leadership passes from one generation to the next.

- ➤ Succession is a key issue: The planning process needs to start early in the successor's life. Tension will invariably develop between the founder and the successor as he/she gains experience.

- ➤ Independent research has shown that there is a lower probability that a third generation will successfully take over the business from the second generation.

In Canada, the Canadian Association of Family Enterprises (CAFE) has been established based on the recognition that families in business often face unique challenges.

CAFE goals are to:

> Perform an advocacy role in building great awareness and understanding of family enterprise issues with governments.

> Facilitate the exchange of ideas and help between individuals involved in family enterprises at all generation levels.

> Provide personal and business support for family members to build executable succession plans[1]

7. CHARACTERISTICS OF SUCCESSFUL START-UPS

To conclude this chapter, we leave you with some observations from successful company owners who have survived the new business growth phase.

> Founders need to have relevant 'hands-on' knowledge and experience at the outset (rather than learning the business as they begin operations.)

> Forge key alliances at an early stage with clients, suppliers, and even competitors (know as "co-petition".) Partner early and partner often.

> Ensure that close management of cash drivers takes place. i.e. prompt account receivable collection, inventory monitoring and advantageous account payable settlement terms .

> Hire talented people and build a committed team. Hire for attitude, train for skill.

> Stick to what you know.

> Focus, focus, focus!

> Develop a strong banking relationship. Keep in touch with your banker on a regular basis.

> Set your goals high. Think like a public company CEO from Day One.

> Fully research your competition. Constantly monitor their performance and initiatives.

➤   Continually update your management skills.

➤   Build a mentoring network that provides objective advice and support.

Useful Web Sites

www.canadaone.com	Canada One – Small business resource directory
www.beyourownboss.org	Be Your Own Boss – extensive search directory
www.ideacafe.com	Idea Café – the fun approach to small business
www.cfa.ca	Canadian Franchise Association
www.thebusinesssource.com	Subscription service providing monthly summaries of current business books
www.cbsc.org	Canada Business Service Centers providing information for start-up or existing companies
www.cafeuc.org	Canadian Association of Family Enterprises (CAFÉ)
www.eventuring.org	On line information for entrepreneurs coded by stages of development

Notes from text.

1. http://www.cafemembers.org/cafenational

NOTES

CHAPTER 9
SOURCES OF EQUITY FUNDING

OVERVIEW

Another crucial element in the development of a new business opportunity is securing sufficient funding to grow and maintain the enterprise. This section examines the equity investment process and how it interfaces with the business life-cycle. Sources of financing, usually only available once a company has reached a more mature growth phase, will be examined in detail in Chapter 11.

While the discussion covers generic start up companies, we will focus on technology based operations since they typically dominate the equity raising process in today's business environment.

The stages of a company's development can be categorized as follows:

> *Seed/Early Stage:* Idea generation and proof of concept.

> *Start Up:* Product development, prototype testing and some initial marketing.

> *First Stage:* Initial production·and sales. Not yet cash flow positive.

> *Second Stage:* Expansion leading to profitable operations and positive cash flow.

> *Maturity:* Product migrations initiated, along with completion of domestic and possibly international expansions.

> *Additional funding:* Obtained from strategic corporate alliances, or IPO. activities.

> *Divestment:* Outside investors or existing management buy either company, division or product line or M&A (Merger and Acquisition)

Figure 9-1

Funding & The Business Life Cycle

Funding Sources ▲	- Personal Savings	- Government Grants - Investment Tax Credits - Family & Friends	- Early Stage Venture Capital - Angel Investors	- Bank Lines of Credit - Leasing - Institutional Venture Capital	- Sub Debt - Private Placements	- Trade Financing - IPOs - Strategic Corporate Alliances	- Outside Investors or Existing Management buy company, division or product line
Company Life Cycle ▲	**Seed Early Stage**	**Start Up**	**First Stage**	**Second Stage**	**Maturity**	**Market Expansion**	**Divestment**
Company Activities ▲	- Initial Market Assessment - Product/Service Idea Generation - Proof of Concept	- Research & Product Development - Prototype Testing - Initial Test Marketing	- Final Product Design - Customer Evaluation & Feedback - Production Facilities Set-Up - Product launch / Initial Production & Sales - Negative Cash Flow	- Expansion Leading to Profitable Operations - Product Refinement - Positive Cash Flow	- Product Migration	- Domestic Expansion - International Expansion	- Merger, Acquisition or Sale

Figure 9-1 (opposite) illustrates the evolution of a technology company and the corresponding sources of funding; commencing with equity and progressing through to more conventional financing vehicles.

Note: Discussion in this chapter relates to the earlier stages of the growth curve which are characterized by greater risk, absence of positive cash flow and the need for equity, NOT debt.

THE EQUITY INVESTMENT PROCESS

1. IDENTIFY FUNDING REQUIREMENTS

Key Points:

- ➤ How much cash is required to fund the venture?

- ➤ How many dollars will be generated internally (from ongoing cash flows) and how many dollars will be required from external (equity) sources?

- ➤ Equity sources will include company founders' cash, credit cards (!) grant programs, research tax credits and outside investors

- ➤ How will the funds be allocated?

  - ♦ working capital
  - ♦ marketing costs
  - ♦ capital assets
  - ♦ research and development

- ➤ When will the funds be advanced? What are the key performance benchmarks or milestones?

- ➤ Will the company be able to generate a sufficient rate of return to reward the investors? (Equity investors will typically look for between 25% and 40% annualized returns over a 3-5 year time horizon.)

  Remember that different investors require different levels of profit sharing, decision-making, and management. There must also be a broad exit strategy envisaged for the investor (IPO, sale of company, management buyback, M&A etc.)

- ➤ Be aware of the 20/60/20 rule

  - 20% are winners
  - 60% are the 'living dead'
  - 20% do not survive

2. Demonstrate Investment Potential

It is critical to understand the risk assessment process that an equity investor will undertake. The following criteria are usually considered:

- What is the company's market opportunity? Are there unique product/service features?

- Is the industry segment known and attractive to the investor (comfort level)?

- Is there evidence of a critical need (and customer acceptance) for the product or service?

- What are the terms of the investment?

  What percentage of the company is being offered? Usually under 50% for early stage companies because the investor does not want to assume day-to-day operational control and associated headaches.

  Having said this, Angels today will structure a deal giving them effective control until certain performance milestones are reached

  What is the estimated value of the business? How was the value derived? How many other investors are at the table?

- Sophisticated investors will be looking to 'add value' to the company, aside from their investment of capital. They may have business contacts, financing relationships or knowledge of potential strategic partnerships that could assist the company in achieving its growth objectives.

- How will return on investment (ROI) requirements be met?

- Will the investor be able to build a solid and enduring relationship with the founder, the target company and its management? This is a critical first step!

- What is the historical and projected operating performance and financial structure?

- Are Intellectual Property interests protected? What other barriers to entry are in place?

- What is the caliber of the management team? What are the specific management skills and attributes in place now and those required for the future?

- Is there a viable exit strategy (three to five years) down the road?

- Is there a Strategic Business plan or Enterprise Review Summary in place?

- How is the investment to be monitored and controlled? (Examples: Board seat, financial statement reporting requirements, capital expenditure approvals, etc.)

> Is there a 'road-map' that details the expected dilution of shareholdings over time? To accomplish this, there will normally be a 'capitalization table' included with the term sheet.

3. COMPLETE A WRITTEN INVESTMENT PROPOSAL

Such a proposal will be built on the primary components of the company business plan, but will be tailored to the equity investment initiative.

Focus should be on the investor's needs and requirements.

Key areas to emphasize

> The market opportunity

> Your management track record (credibility and experience).

> Equity stake available to the investor

- ♦ Amount
- ♦ Investment terms/duration
- ♦ Use of proceeds

> Revenue/earnings growth projections (to meet investor's ROI)

> Anticipated exit strategies for the investor

> Obtain feedback from outside professional advisors.

> Ensure confidentiality.

> Ensure compliance with all legal and regulatory requirements.

A useful document to accomplish this step is an Enterprise Review Summary (ERS), which is a concise three-to-four page summary that describes the funding opportunity for the investor. This concept is covered in greater detail in Chapter 13 – Strategic Business Plans.

4. IDENTIFY POTENTIAL INVESTORS

The following categories of equity investor can be identified, beginning with the earliest players that come to the table:

➤ *Founder's cash*

> Personal cash injections from savings accounts, securities, home equity sources, etc. Credit cards are increasingly being 'maxed out' to generate the required start-up capital (not for the faint of heart and certainly not recommended as a funding source).

➤ *Friends and family (F & F)*

> Also known as love money, seed money or guilt money.

> Dollar amounts are generally small (up to $100,000), with proceeds typically used to test concepts, initiate product development, and market research.

> This type of investor will typically invest in 'you' the founder as opposed to the business opportunity.

➤ *Angel investors*

> ◆ Angels are generally individuals who maintain a low profile and are usually contacted through professional advisors.

> ◆ These are sophisticated investors who will complete extensive due diligence, with initial investment amounts in the $50,000 to $750,000 range.

> ◆ They typically look for 35-45% ROI (Return on Investment) within 3-5 years.

> ◆ Angels will usually bring experience, contacts and strategic advice to the table.

> ◆ They are more likely to become involved in an earlier stage company and one with global potential.

> ◆ Tend to invest in local companies (within a 50 Km radius).

➤ *Government-backed programs*

> Some examples:

> The Business Development Bank (BDC) provides a spectrum of quasi equity programs ranging from $100,000 to $1 million for expansion and market development projects that usually require some form of equity matching.

The Industrial Research Assistance Program (IRAP): This program provides match-funding grants (50:50) through the National Research Council.

> *Venture Capital firms*

Seldom work with new startups and are more likely to seek out existing companies that need assistance in ramping up revenue and achieving positive cash flow generation.

These investors will be professionals with extensive experience and contacts, looking for annualized returns in the 30+% range.

Investment size will range from $2 to $5 million.

These firms tend to 'travel in herds' and will often syndicate to achieve relative safety in numbers.

Tend to invest in 'what's hot'.

Scalability is important to this type of investor. A business that is able to add new clients with little extra effort and cost is said to be scalable.

> *Institutional investors*

Provide equity to medium-sized businesses with investment requirements usually in the $10 million+ range.

Example: Bank subsidiaries (i.e., TD Capital)

> *Strategic Corporate investors*

These consist of strategic alliances or corporate partnerships involving established, successful companies that are looking to gain new product and market access or exposure to new technologies.

> *Public Offerings*

Initial Public Offerings (IPOs) involve raising additional capital through a formalized share offering process on public exchanges. In Canada – TSX exchanges In USA, through 'over the counter' exchanges or NASDAQ.

This process usually takes place *after* a number of 'private rounds' of equity investments. Timing is crucial from both the investment climate (external) and the company's (internal) cash generation performance.

Further dilution of the founding shareholder's interests will take place, along with new accountability to other stakeholders such as public shareholders, regulators, etc.)

A prospectus, available to public shareholders, provides a detailed description of the company and the investment opportunity. Regulators provide tight control over the process to protect the public.

Underwriters sell the stock through the selected stock market after deciding on the issue price based upon orders booked from retail and institutional investors.

The process is very expensive and requires a huge time and financial commitment. There will be substantial accounting requirements prior to the IPO that need to be met.

The listing process will entail costs between 6-8% of the issue which will be retained by the underwriters. Intensive road shows and lengthy investor relations initiatives add to the overall cost.

One unexpected outcome arising from an IPO is that suppliers, customers and competition suddenly have a detailed update on your financial performance (historical and projected) and your strategic plans by way of the prospectus that is issued to potential investors.

If the IPO process is successful, there will be significant gains in credibility, access to international capital markets and the ability to offer more liquid stock options to attract top-tier employees.

Given the complexity of the process, it is crucial to ask this question a number of times … is the company ready to go public?

RESOURCES AVAILABLE TO LOCATE INVESTORS

- Directories or Associations (Canadian Venture Capital Association)
- Industry and local technology associations
- Professional advisors/mentors
- Government sources (Federal/Provincial)
- Internet (Example: garage.com – Hewlett Packard's VC web site)

SELECTING A POTENTIAL INVESTOR – KEY ISSUES

You have to understand that this is a *two way* process. It is essential to assess the potential investors' background and capabilities. They will be completing extensive due diligence on you – the investee – the same process should be undertaken by you!

Consider the following:

- ➤ Character, reputation and credibility.

- ➤ Commitment and financial staying power (deep pockets). Will the investors be involved and have strong links to the next round of funding?

- ➤ Do they have the ability to bring other resources to the table, such as market and/or competitor knowledge? Do they understand prevailing industry and technology issues?

- ➤ What is their past track record? Have there been any problem investments?

- ➤ Compatibility. Is there a shared personal and business vision?

- ➤ References?

5. GETTING FACE-TO-FACE WITH POTENTIAL INVESTORS

Some tips and tactics to achieve an effective live presentation:

- ➤ Practice the presentation beforehand – there are no second chances.

- ➤ Determine who from your team will be the presenter. This person should ideally be the company founder or CEO who is able to communicate his or her passion, commitment and staying power to the potential investor audience.

- ➤ Know your audience and tailor the message accordingly. Investors, corporate strategic partners or potential clients will require different presentations.

- ➤ Address the audience directly and establish eye contact. Do not read from previously prepared notes.

- ➤ Quickly arrive at the company's value proposition and uniqueness. It is critical that the audiences understand and become excited at the opportunity facing them (reaching for their wallets).

- ➤ Seasoned investors and strategic partners will 'bet on the jockey, not the horse'. You need to demonstrate which key management people are now in place along with their strengths and experience. Investors or potential partners will not invest on the promise of hiring key personnel in the future.

- ➤ Product functionality does not have to be demonstrated at the presentation. Its effectiveness is a given and will be validated by a due-diligence process completed at a later date. Instead, focus on the market opportunity.

➤ Support the presentation with sales or marketing brochures which further illustrate the market potential.

➤ PowerPoint presentations are now the standard. While overheads are '1940's technology', they can be kept in reserve in case software or projector problems occur.

SOME (HARD-NOSED) QUESTIONS THAT YOU WILL BE ASKED AT THE PRESENTATION

➤ What is your background and track record?

➤ What is your financial commitment?

➤ Do you have a well-defined market niche that you can dominate (uniqueness)?

➤ Do you understand your customer and required sales channels?

➤ Detail your management team's experience and technical capabilities?

➤ How will the requested investment funds be used?

➤ What are your revenue and earnings growth assumptions?

➤ What is your competitive advantage? Who are your competitors? What are their relative strengths and weaknesses? Do you have any intellectual property or other barriers to entry?

➤ What steps have you taken to protect your intellectual property and ensure exclusivity with no strings attached? Were you working for someone else when you first developed the product or technology?

➤ What ROI will be achieved over the life of the investment? Is there a viable exit strategy?

➤ How will the proceeds of this investment influence your existing business strategy?

➤ What are your motivations – ego or wealth creation? (Ego implies a desire to 'stay at the helm' at all costs, even though the ship is sinking.)

➤ What are your weaknesses? This is a tough question that tests your willingness to disclose information. It is critical that you outline any challenges or obstacles frankly if you are to win the confidence of the potential investors.

➤ The initial introduction should take place through a respected intermediary (accountant, lawyer, commercial banker, local technology association.)

➤ Investors will complete an extensive due diligence review which will involve the following:

- ◆ checking your references
- ◆ reviewing legal agreements and bank authorities
- ◆ completing a facilities tour
- ◆ obtaining credit bureau reports
- ◆ analyzing historical financial statements
- ◆ reviewing financial projections and assumptions

A due diligence information package will address the above points and should be prepared for the investors. They may elect to have some of their due diligence completed by an independent third party assessment report.

6. NEGOTIATING AND CLOSING THE DEAL

Key Points:

➤ The personal relationship between the investor and investee (founder) must be solid and enduring.

➤ The investor will issue a preliminary Term Sheet outlining the terms of the deal. This document needs to be carefully reviewed with your accountant and your lawyer.

➤ Further due diligence will take place by the investor prior to the completion of formal documentation and the shareholder agreement. This is an essential document which requires careful review with your legal advisors.

➤ A wide range of stakeholders has to be considered at this crucial stage so the closing process is invariably protracted (lots of lawyers).

➤ Time considerations:

Raising capital is a time-consuming and often frustrating effort. No matter when you think it should be completed, it will take longer due to unforeseen delays, especially the preparation of legal documentation and term sheet negotiations.

A key insight: Start early and seek funding assistance before you need it. Never negotiate a term sheet when you are cash strapped

7. VALUATION ISSUES

In the previous chapter, company valuations based on 'going concern' criteria were discussed. With start-up companies, there have been no sales, stabilized earnings or cash flow that would allow you to perform a realistic valuation calculation.

An investor will be prepared to commit some new venture capital to a deal but will also want to attain a meaningful shareholding in the company.

The following methodology describes how such an equity stake is derived:

The concept here is to project the valuation process 'into the future' by completing some simple future value calculations. (It should be noted that the same % ownership result can also be obtained by taking future earnings and completing a *present* value calculation.)

Assumptions

1. The enterprise requires $500,000 for new product and market development.

2. The investor, after assessing the venture's risk profile, determines that a 35% rate of return, compounded annually over Five years, is required.

3. The company's financial projections estimate EBIT at $800,000 achieved at the end of Year Five. These projections have been carefully assessed and stress tested by the investor.

4. The investor's research indicates a current Industry price/earnings multiple in the 8x range.

Calculation

➤ The Future value of the company in Year Five based on the price/earnings multiple and forecast EBIT.

$800,000 x 8   =$6.4 million

➤ The future value of the investor's $500,000 investment, compounded (monthly) at 35% through to Year Five   =$2.24 million

➤ Equity stake   = $\underline{\$2.24}$ =35%
                               $6.40

Therefore, the investor would negotiate a 35%+ stake in the company. The owner would retain 65% having received a $500,000 equity injection to expedite product and market development.

If the company has a proven history of sales and positive earnings, potential investors would likely use a revenue multiple model (1 to 2 times annual revenues) based upon similar sale transactions observed in the specific industry sector.

Useful Web Sites

www.vef.org	Vancouver Enterprise Forum – Money links.
www.strategis.ic.gc.ca/sources	Industry Canada Strategis web site providing an excellent guide to business management resources including investment guidelines and success stories
www.businessfinance.com	Business capital search engine (USA)
www.wofund.com	GrowthWorks Ltd. (Working Opportunity Fund) – venture capital reference site
www.ventureswest.com	Ventures West technology venture capital reference site
www.ventureplan.com	Business valuations
www.yaletown.com	Yaletown Venture Partners
www.angelinvestmentnetwork.ca	Canadian Angel Network
www.angelforum.org	B.C Angel Forum

NOTES

CHAPTER 10
MANAGING GROWTH

OVERVIEW

As companies grow and mature, a transition from entrepreneurial management to professional management is required. Entrepreneurial management is characterized by centralized, often solo, decision making, an informal style, control system and structure.

Professional management involves more delegated decision-making authority and use of formalized control systems. In this chapter, opportunities to grow the business are examined.

It is important to note that growth requires further qualification. Is a company seeking growth in market share? Revenues? Margin? Earnings? Or a combination of all these?

The following areas are covered:

1. Growth and development strategies

2. Diversification – product or market growth?

3. International expansion

1. GROWTH AND DEVELOPMENT STRATEGIES

Here are some questions that help to assess a company's growth potential:

➤ What is the profile of current clients? Will they be the same in the future?

➤ How do you access clients? Can different or supplemental channels be used in the future?

> Who are the competition now and will new competitors join them in the future?

> Is there potential to enhance gross and net profit margins?

> Are there partnering or alliance opportunities that will build market share, promote product migration or build economies of scale?

Strategy comes from the Greek language and translates as 'the art of generalship'. The four strategies below are prevalent in most expanding and medium-sized companies. The key is to recognize which particular strategy provides your company with a distinct competitive advantage.

A. DIFFERENTIATION

Companies can be 'different' in many ways by undertaking strategies that make them distinct from their competition.

A key concept is that a company needs to craft a strategy of being unique in the eyes of its customers – it has to incorporate attributes into its product or service offerings that separate it from competitor offerings

Some ways a company can set itself apart from the competition are:

Product Features

> Can new features or attributes be developed that will attract potential buyers and meet their unmet needs? (e.g. one stop shopping at Home Depot)

> Can the product be improved by multiple features? (e.g. Microsoft Office)

Product Packaging

> Consider *how* the product will be sold and what types of bundled features and services can be offered. (All-inclusive resort vacations).

Product Distribution

> Accurate order completion, fast delivery. (Dell Computer)

Product Quality

➢ Quality is often in the eye of the beholder – perception can be reality.

➢ The following checklist of quality characteristics serves to differentiate your operations from the competition:

- ◆ durability and reliability (e.g. Duracell batteries)
- ◆ safety (e.g. Michelin Tires)
- ◆ consistent performance (e.g. South West Airlines)
- ◆ prestige (e.g. Cadillac, Mercedes-Benz)

Service Quality

➢ A similar list of quality characteristics can be developed for service industries:

- ◆ awareness of client needs and wants
- ◆ dependability
- ◆ customer service
- ◆ proven reputation
- ◆ integrity and trust
- ◆ responsiveness

B. LOW-COST LEADERSHIP

➢ Involves an intensive review of all company operations to identify and eliminate unnecessary costs.

➢ Is most effective in industries where consumer-buying decisions are price sensitive.

➢ Product simplicity can be developed by reducing cost inputs (materials, labor), which translates to a lower unit price. Such stripped-down products and services can be observed in most industry sectors. *Examples:*

- ◆ Discount airlines: West Jet, SouthWest Airlines.
- ◆ Discount brokerages: TD Waterhouse, Charles Schwab.
- ◆ Warehouse stores: Canadian Tire,

➢ To maximize cost advantages, a useful approach is to examine the company's value chain – a linked set of activities and functions of that culminate in the delivery of a product or service to the end-user. An example would be a shift to e-commerce by using online order processing as opposed to face-to-face order taking.

> Implementation is the key. To assume a low-cost leadership role, the company's organizational structure, reward systems and employee culture need to reflect the vision of a lean and effective organization.

C. FOCUS STRATEGIES

Focus strategies that are aimed at either low-cost or differentiation opportunities involve concentrating on a smaller piece of the potential revenue pie.

Examples:

> *Specialty products* that deliver non-standard items, i.e., specialty, antique bathtubs.

> *Niches.* These are small, carefully defined market segments providing opportunities to exceed client expectations, i.e., small, up-scale eco-tourism resorts.

> *Limited geographic territory.* Focus on local or regional markets that have been overlooked by larger companies.

D. INTEGRATION

There are two types of integration – Vertical and Horizontal.

1. **Vertical:** Opportunities to expand arise within a company's own (vertical) industry sector.

   - *Backward integration* – extends business activities 'back' in the supply chain towards raw materials and sources of supply.
   - *Forward integration* – extends business activities 'forward' in the supply chain and closer to the company's marketplace; i.e., a food wholesaler establishing a retail outlet (taking care to ensure there is no direct competition with existing retail clients).

2. **Horizontal:** Involves the assumption of increased control over competitors in a similar market. This usually translates to a merger or takeover which can be friendly (rescue or collaboration) or unfriendly (corporate raid).

2. DIVERSIFICATION – PRODUCT OR MARKET GROWTH?

Having reviewed various development strategies that can assist a company to grow with a tangible game plan; it is also instructive to assess growth opportunities from a product and market standpoint.

A Growth Directions Matrix (originally developed by Igor Ansoff)[1] is an effective and graphic method that allows the summary of company product or market growth opportunities. This illustrated by Figure 10 -1 (below).

Figure 10 -1

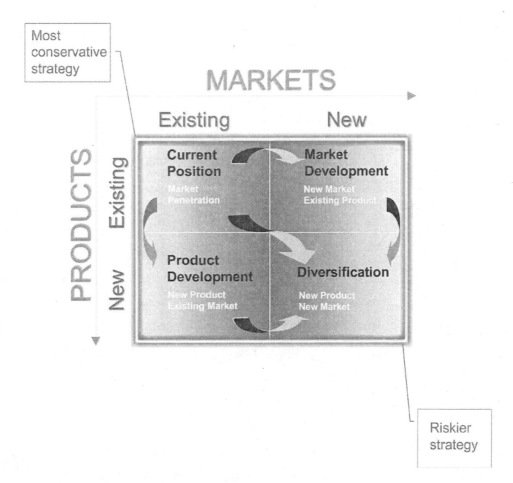

Consider the four options:

1) Existing Products and Markets

- ♦ The status quo – which involves maintaining steady growth, 'doing everything a little better, every day'.
- ♦ Growth in this sector is achieved by adopting a *market penetration* strategy, striving to increase market share for existing products or services.

2) New Market, Existing Product

- ♦ A *market development* strategy is implemented which involves finding a fresh market for existing products or services by either:
  - – expanding geographically (regional or international expansion)
  - – seeking new groups of customers
  - – growing existing channel/distribution partnerships

A useful checklist when considering the move into new, potential market segments is shown below:

- ➢ How do you define the new market segment(s)?
- ➢ Are the market segments 'emerging' as opposed to 'established'?
- ➢ Is there good 'bowling pin' potential – adjacent, closely related, market niches that can also be targeted?
- ➢ How will a compelling 'value-added differentiation' be created for these new buyers?
- ➢ Are there any direct competitors or near substitutes?
- ➢ What is the expected revenue/cost structure and break-even for the new segment?
- ➢ What is the 'brand message' – is it an understandable buying proposition?
- ➢ Will there be a compelling tag line that conveys features and benefits?
- ➢ How easy or complex is the buyers' purchase decision and mode of payment?
- ➢ How do you build market awareness?
- ➢ What will be the most effective distribution channel?
- ➢ What are the best promotional tactics – tradeshows, catalogues etc?
- ➢ Are there 'follow on' expansion opportunities, domestic or international?
- ➢ Do potential alliance or partnering opportunities exist within these new market segments?

3) New Products, Existing Markets

- ◆ Involves the development of entirely new products (or revising additional features for existing products) that are targeted at existing customers.

The following checklist assists with the *new product assessment* process:

- ➤ How would you describe the product or service – in a 15 second elevator pitch?
- ➤ What is it going to do? What will it look like?
- ➤ Would I buy it? If not, what would induce me to do so?
- ➤ What unmet need or want does it address? What problem does it solve?
- ➤ Define the most valuable and most used features that it will have?
- ➤ What are the costs to take it to market?
- ➤ Define the timeframe before first clients use the product or service?
- ➤ How will it be delivered to the end user?
- ➤ How has the price point been justified (payback on the development costs)?
- ➤ What are the product or service design/development resources required?
- ➤ Identify the testing (pilot, prototype) and market feedback process?
- ➤ If a product, what are functionality and durability requirements?
- ➤ How will quality be demonstrated to the user?
- ➤ Will it be possible to make incremental improvements to the product/service?
- ➤ Are there any future 'bundling' opportunities? Bundling is the ability to sell the product or service along with other products/services as a 'bundle'.
- ➤ If a product, is there a need for a follow up service component?
- ➤ Are intellectual property (I.P) rights fully protected and documented – how easy is it to replicate?
- ➤ Is there a need to partner with other entities within the supply chain to provide a 'whole product solution'?

4) New Product, New Markets

- ◆ This strategy involves setting off in a new direction and attempting to create new products in fresh markets. This is known as 'conglomerate diversification.'

- Becoming a 'new product, new market' pioneer entails *significant risks!* Before undertaking this strategy, a comprehensive review and assessment of company internal resources needs to take place to ensure capability and staying power are available to launch this new venture.

The preceeding four options each have different needs and cost implications. The 'status quo' is the least risky per se but keeps the firm stagnant and may lead to its costly and eventual decline. Offering existing products or services in new markets or new products or services in existing markets is less risky and costly than an incursion with new product/services in new markets.

MANAGING MULTIPLE MARKETS AND PRODUCTS

As a company grows, different product lines and markets will unfold. To assess and monitor this portfolio of different activities, General Electric developed the Strategic Business Unit (SBU) concept. SBUs form component parts of a company with each unit having its own products, markets and competitors.

Figure 10-2

BCG GROWTH-SHARE GRID
Relative Market Share

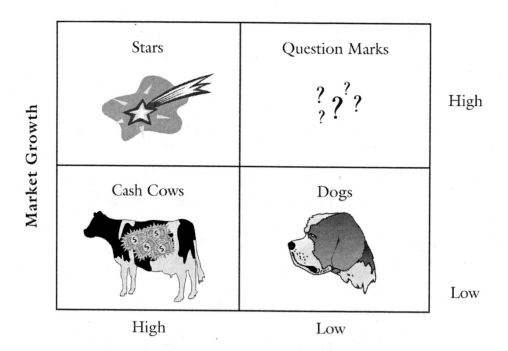

Source: Boston Consulting Group Inc. Reprinted with permission from BCG Global Services, Boston, MA 02109

SBUs will either be generators or users of cash. A *Portfolio Growth Share Grid* (developed by the Boston Consulting Group) provides a simple portfolio analysis based upon market growth and relative market share. This is illustrated by Figure 10-2 (below) along with a brief review of the different SBU categories.

TYPES OF SBUS

Question Marks

  ➤ Experience low market share in high-growth markets and are sometimes referred to as 'problem children.'

  ➤ Require significant cash resources to keep afloat in the hope that they can build market share over time, that is turn them into 'stars'.

Stars

  ➤ Have achieved high market share in high-growth markets. They have strong appetites for cash (to fund continuous expansion) but, on balance, tend to be self supporting from a cash flow standpoint.

Cash Cows

  ➤ Have established major market share in low-growth segments with significant cash being generated from operations.

  ➤ Products are well known and established. Their low-growth markets are mature.

  ➤ Surplus cash proceeds are often used to feed promising SBUs (question marks) elsewhere in the company.

Dogs

  ➤ Deliver low market share in low-growth markets.

  ➤ Are often net users of cash.

  ➤ Tend to be marginal businesses that need to be divested or possibly restructured or repositioned.

3. INTERNATIONAL EXPANSION

OVERVIEW

With global markets growing and domestic competition becoming more intense, many companies look to explore international expansion and exporting opportunities.

Benefits of such expansion initiatives include:

➤ Potential to expand market share

➤ Increase revenues and earnings

➤ New alliance/partnering opportunities

➤ Acquiring new customers and applications for existing products

Moving into the international marketplace is a complex and time-consuming, long-term process. A detailed analysis is beyond the scope of this text, however we have summarized a few key issues that will assist the evaluation process.

EXTERNAL EVALUATION

➤ Critically assess the political and economic health of the target country.

♦ Is there potential for political unrest or a change in trade regulations?

♦ What is the current inflation rate and trade balance?

♦ Assess the target country tax regimes and any product/service compliance requirements.

➤ Are you planning to target national or regional markets within the foreign country?

➤ Does the international expansion strategy entail a significant change in customer profile within your target offshore market?

➤ How will the goods or services be delivered to your new customers?

♦ What are the cost/timing implications?

♦ What will be the shipping and insurance costs?

INTERNAL EVALUATION

➤ Do you have a strong equity and working capital position to back up a long-term export venture?

➤ Will the international venture have a negative impact on your existing domestic business?

➤ Do you have sufficient employee talent and resources to open up new markets and, at the same time, look after the existing domestic market?

> *Remember* – take care of your existing markets/customers first!

➤ Do you have a sound relationship with your bank? Do they have a trade finance department to guide you?

➤ Have you completed a market development plan which addresses the following issues:

> How big is the international market?
>
> What will be your estimated share of the target market?
>
> What was the basis of your market research?
>
> How closely does your expertise and competence compare to other competitors?
>
> Does the competition consist of one or two 'gorrilla' or number of similar size firms?
>
> What is your expected gross profit margin and what are the overhead cost implications? OK

➤ What will be your entry strategy into the foreign market?

- Use intermediaries such as agents, foreign distributors or manufacturers' representatives?
- Assuming a subcontracting relationship working for a host country company?
- Direct interaction as an exporter with the foreign customer?
- Establishing an offshore branch office or subsidiary operation?
- Forging a joint venture with another firm to penetrate a specific foreign market?
- Licensing products, services or technology to an offshore firm?

EXPORT FINANCING

Three key issues to consider:

- ➤ Getting paid
- ➤ Managing credit (receivable) risk
- ➤ Managing currency risk

1) MANAGING PAYMENT RISK

There is a spectrum of options ranging from secure to risky from an exporter's perspective.

The most secure option for the exporter is *cash in advance,* which obviously eliminates all risk of nonpayment. However, in reality, few foreign buyers are willing to pay full cash up front.

The most risky option is the *open account transaction* where the exporter has the sole responsibility in determining the ability of the purchaser to pay. The exporter must finance the transaction with its own funds, ship the goods and then await payment.

There is a 'middle ground' whereby a *letter of credit* (L/C) is established via the exporter's bank, which is effectively, eliminates any credit risk associated with the buyer.

2) MANAGING CREDIT RISK

Other than generic Letters of Credit, there are other ways to ensure payment, such as:

- ➤ Insurance: Export receivables are insured by organizations like the Export Development Corporation (EDC).

- ➤ CCC (Canadian Credit Corporation): Provides foreign buyers with a guarantee of contract completion. There is also a PPP (Progress Payment Program) that allows exporters to obtain pre-shipment financing.

3) MANAGING CURRENCY RISK

Foreign exchange rate risk can be hedged through your bank by establishing a forward exchange contract. This contract effectively hedges the risk of adverse foreign exchange fluctuations (the value of importers currency relative to the Canadian dollar.)

We recommend the TD trade finance web site, which provides an excellent online seminar on export financing issues.

USEFUL WEB SITES

www.exportsource.gc.ca	Guide for Canadian exporters
www.brs-inc.com	Business resource software for start up and growth companies
www.edc-see.ca	Export Development Corporation providing trade finance services to Canadian exporters and investors
www.tdglobaltradefinance.com	GTF crash course on Trade Finance

Notes from text.

1. H.Igor Ansoff, *Corporate Strategy*, Penguin, Harmondsworth

NOTES

CHAPTER 11
SOURCES OF DEBT FINANCING

OVERVIEW

In this chapter, sources of debt financing are reviewed. While there are no hard and fast rules, early stage companies will usually be funded from equity sources (owner, seed capital, angels, etc.) Debt financing is invariably difficult to obtain.

Why is this?

The primary reason is cash flow. A company should be able to demonstrate that it can generate *sustainable* cash flow from its operations in order to service (pay interest) and repay any debt obligations. Many early stage companies struggle to become cash flow positive and do not need a 'heavy backpack' of debt to burden their operations.

As a company matures and builds a solid track record of revenues, earnings and cash flow generation, a wide array of financing vehicles become available to them. This growth can be funded by *both* debt and additional equity streams like venture capital rounds.

The second part of this chapter provides strategic tips that will assist you in negotiating mutually beneficial opportunities with your bank.

SECTION ONE

TYPES OF DEBT FINANCING

In this section, the following sources of financing are presented:

1. Commercial banks.

2. Government initiatives.

3. Other types of debt financing.

1. COMMERCIAL BANKS

Commercial banks are the primary source of debt financing for small- and medium-sized companies. The different types of loans are detailed below:

A. OPERATING (REVOLVING) LINES OF CREDIT

Purpose:

> ➤ To finance short-term working capital needs (accounts receivable collection and inventory purchases).

Features:

> ➤ An authorized dollar limit is established based on a forecast of peak cash needs in any one month of the year.

> ➤ Borrowings are usually on demand, with a floating interest rate established at an agreed-upon percentage over the prevailing Prime rate (e.g., Prime + 1%).

> ➤ Operating borrowings are usually margined. You can only borrow up to a specified percentage of accounts receivable and inventories on your books as at a specific month end. e.g., 75% of Accounts Receivable under 60 days, plus 50% Inventory at estimated cost.

> ➤ Security generally consists of a GSA (General Security Agreement) which provides the bank with a specific legal charge (claim) over your accounts receivable, inventory and (potentially) other company assets (known as a 'floating charge').

B. TERM LOANS

Purpose:

> ➤ Extended for equipment purchases with the term of the loan (three to seven years) matched to the expected life of the asset.

Features:

> ➤ Available on a floating or fixed-rate basis.

> ➤ Security will consist of a fixed, specific charge over the asset being acquired.

> ➤ Financing in 60% to 70% range is usually negotiable.

C. COMMERCIAL MORTGAGES

Purpose:

> ➤ To assist with the purchase/refinancing of commercial real estate.

Features:

> ➤ Usually available on a fixed-rate basis. Interest rates are locked in for one to seven year terms. Amortization periods are typically between 15 and 25 years depending on the quality and location of the real estate asset.

> ➤ Financing is available between 60% to 75% of current appraised value.

> ➤ Security consists of a first mortgage over the real estate asset along with an assignment of rents and fire insurance. Personal or corporate guarantees may also be required.

D. LETTERS OF CREDIT

Available for exporting or importing situations:

> ➤ Exporter wishes to sell goods or services but wants the assurance of payment before commencing production and delivery.

> ➤ Offshore importer wishes to purchase goods or services but does not wish to pay until shipping and title documents are received and are in good order.

E. BRIDGE LOANS

Interim financing is provided on a short-term basis to cover project costs pending inflow of sales proceeds or long-term financing.

Example: A real estate construction project (townhouses) is to be built. Construction and interest costs will be financed by the bank pending sale of the townhouse units.

F. CREDIT CARDS

Expense and purchasing cards for the business.

G. PERSONAL LOANS

Available to the company owner to raise additional funds and then inject into the company by way of a shareholder loan.

2. GOVERNMENT INITIATIVES

A. CANADA SMALL BUSINESS FINANCING PROGRAM (CSBFP)

Features:

- ➢ CSBFP loans are available from banks for amounts of up to $250,000.
- ➢ 85% of the value of the loan is guaranteed by the federal government.
- ➢ Loan proceeds are used for the acquisition of land, buildings, and machinery. (Note: this program does not cover inventory financing).
- ➢ Fixed or floating rates (Prime + 3% including a loan loss reserve premium)
- ➢ 2% fee loan registration fee.
- ➢ Terms up to 10 years.

B. INDUSTRIAL RESEARCH ASSOCIATION PROGRAMS (IRAP)

Administered through the National Research Council. IRAP programs provide financial assistance (on a match-funding basis) to technology companies for R&D and new technology assessments.

C. SCIENTIFIC RESEARCH AND EXPERIMENTAL DEVELOPMENT (SR & ED)

> ➤ SR &ED tax rebates are available to qualifying technology companies.

D. PROGRAM FOR EXPERIMENTAL MARKET DEVELOPMENT (PEMD)

Financial assistance is provided to companies to attend international trade shows.

3. OTHER TYPES OF DEBT FINANCING

A. LEASING

> ➤ Available from banks, equipment manufacturers and lease financing companies for business equipment and larger ticket items (e.g., specialized manufacturing equipment).

> ➤ Lease terms typically run from 36 to 60 months and cover 100% cost of the asset being leased.

Benefits:

> ➤ Preserves working capital (cash) for expansion purposes.

> ➤ Leaves operating credit lines available for non-fixed asset financing needs.

> ➤ Provides a hedge against equipment obsolescence.

Note: It is important to obtain professional advice from your accountant to ensure that there are favorable tax consequences arising from leasing versus borrowing to purchase.

Figure 11-1 (next page) summarizes the buying versus leasing decision and the resultant ownership relationships.

Figure 11-1

BUY OR LEASE?

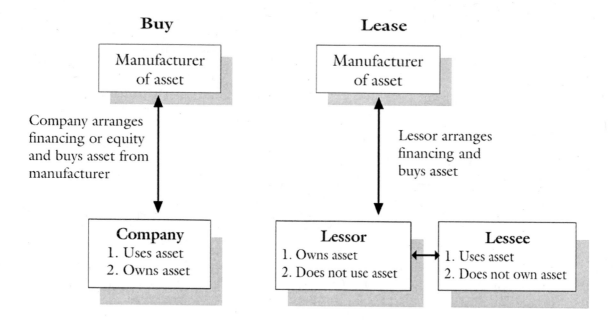

B. FLOOR PLAN FINANCING

➤ Loans provided by manufacturers which allow retailers or distributors to acquire product (inventory) and make it available for sale. The floor loan is repaid from the product sales proceeds.

C. MEZZANINE FINANCING

Also known as a subordinated debt ('sub debt'). This is a form of financing that falls between traditional debt and equity on the balance sheet.

Sub debt is a blend of equity and conventional debt with no reliance on collateral assets, yet requiring regular monthly interest and principal payments.

Features:

➤ Relatively high interest rates (12% to 18%) provide the mezzanine lender with a reasonable return relative to the risk profile of the company.

➤ An equity component, usually warrants, is sometimes required, enabling the lender to acquire future equity (15% to 25%) of the company.

➤ Deal size – in Canada, usually up to $5 million.

➤ Term – usually up to five years with monthly blended payments. Seasonal payments, cash sweeps or balloon payment mechanisms can also be set up.

➤ Security – General Security Agreement (GSA) providing a floating charge of the business assets, subordinated to the senior lender. Limited personal guarantees along with an assignment of key person insurance is usually required.

Benefits:

➤ Targeted at rapid growth companies that need supplemental funding over and above traditional sources of debt and equity.

➤ Sub debt lenders look primarily at the company's cash flow and 'enterprise value' for payment and return on equity as opposed to more traditional lenders who derive comfort from the book value of assets, which have been pledged as collateral.

➤ Cheaper than pure equity investments and more flexible than conventional debt.

➤ Board seats are not usually required.

➤ Improved working capital position

➤ Uses of sub debt can include:

- ◆ Significant marketing expenditures
- ◆ Management buyouts
- ◆ New product development
- ◆ Strategic acquisitions
- ◆ Typical underwriting criteria:

➤ Strong management in place with a significant ownership stake in the business.

➤ The company is experiencing strong revenue growth (minimum 20% per year).

➤ Cash flow positive (EBITDA) demonstrated over a minimum one year period.

➤ Other sophisticated investors (venture capital firms) and lenders (banks) are also participating.

➤ Healthy relationship with senior lender plus adequate operating credits in place.

➤ A defined exit strategy is in place (i.e., IPO, re-financing or sale of company).

D. RESTRUCTURING LOAN PAYMENTS

➤ 'Interest only' through slow cash flow periods.

➤ Balloon payments at the end of a loan term, thereby lowering prior principal monthly payments.

➤ Seasonal 'lump sum' principal payments.

E. BOOTSTRAP FINANCING

Bootstrap financing arises when a venture is launched with modest personal funds and is then 'bootstrapped' up the growth curve by implementing creative survival strategies. Close attention to cash flow and cash resources is a key feature of this process.

Some strategies from the world of bootstrap finance:

Factoring

➤ A company (factor) purchases your accounts receivable, advancing 70% to 90% of a specific invoice amount.

➤ Servicing fees (2% value of the receivable) are charged along with an interest rate (Prime + 3% plus) on funds advanced prior to the collection of the invoice.

➤ This can be an alternative source of financing for companies that do not yet qualify for operating credit lines.

➤ No additional liabilities are added to the Balance Sheet (existing accounts receivable are merely discounted by the factoring company).

➤ The accelerated receipt of cash can relieve seasonal cash flow pressures and allow companies to take advantage of trade discounts from suppliers and/or special product purchase opportunities.

Customer Credit

➤ It may be possible to negotiate with your clients that they provide advance payments in the early stages of a particular project.

Supplier Credit

➤ Trade credit terms can be negotiated with suppliers, often with long lead times to allow for seasonal impacts on the cash flow cycle (another cash driver strategy).

Landlord Credit

> ➤ Financial assistance from your landlord (assuming that the premises are rented) may be available to complete additional leasehold improvements. Temporary deferral of monthly rent during a tight cash flow period may also be negotiable.

Other Options

> ➤ Expand slowly and carefully. While 'first mover advantage' may be lost, the slow and steady approach to expansion means less pressure on limited working capital resources.

> ➤ Minimize unnecessary capital expenditures.

> ➤ Have employees accept stock options or profit sharing in lieu of industry standard wages until the business becomes more established.

> ➤ With custom orders, negotiate a 30% - 60% - 10% payment structure from customers: 30% up front, 60% upon delivery and a 10% holdback to cover performance issues.

> ➤ Try to acquire a 'lighthouse client': a well-known and credible industry leader who will serve as an attractive reference to other potential clients, corporate strategic partners and investors.

SECTION TWO

DEALING WITH BANKS

In this section, the following issues are reviewed:

1. How to build a strong relationship with your bank

2. The loan approval process – some key issues

3. How bankers 'risk assess' your company

4. Due diligence considerations

5. A sample financing commitment letter

1. HOW TO BUILD A STRONG RELATIONSHIP WITH YOUR BANKER – FIVE KEY STEPS

LOCATE THE RIGHT BANKER

If you are seeking a new bank, remember that the key to an enduring relationship will be the *individual* commercial banker.

Questions to ask:

➤ What are your qualifications and length of commercial lending experience?

➤ Do you have a team approach to commercial banking relationships? Who provides ongoing support to you and to whom do you report?

➤ Provide an overview of your commercial loan portfolio. Which industries do you specialize in and where have you had the most success?

➤ How important is commercial banking to your bank?

DEMONSTRATE CREDIBILITY AND RELIABILITY

➤ Through business plan presentations, demonstrate your intimate knowledge of company operations, major competitors and industry opportunities and threats.

➤ Under promise and over deliver.

➤ Provide credible, accurate and timely financial information as part of your monthly reporting and annual review process.

➤ Anticipate financing needs early (i.e., temporary bulges, new capital financing needs).

➤ Invite your banker to your place of business and provide a tour and an introduction to key personnel.

BUILD A TEAM OF PROFESSIONAL ADVISORS

➤ Your banker will want to know who provides you with accounting, legal, and strategic advice. He/she will likely know these professionals personally.

➤ Do not hesitate to involve your accountant in any complex or difficult loan negotiations.

COMMUNICATE

> ➤ Keep your banker informed regarding any issues (positive or negative) that might impact your business operations or industry segment.

> ➤ Report bad news or deteriorating trends **early,** along with a plan of action to deal with them. Avoid providing your bank with unpleasant surprises.

> ➤ Let the bank know whether or not they are meeting your expectations. Get issues out on the table quickly.

SEEK OUT OTHER RESOURCES

Your bank is far more than a place to borrow money. Other areas where support can be provided include:

> ➤ Cash management services:
>
>   ♦ Allow the monitoring of account activities and transfer of funds via the Internet.
>   ♦ B2B services: Electronic portals that allow you to expand supplier/ client contacts.
>   ♦ Pay interest income on commercial deposit balances.

> ➤ Trade finance: Export/import assistance.

> ➤ Foreign exchange: Currency conversions and hedging strategies.

> ➤ Interest rate hedging: For larger clients, strategies are available that swap floating for fixed interest rates, and establish caps/floors to minimize future interest rate fluctuations.

Your banker also runs a business within a business with a portfolio of commercial clients that forms part of the bank's overall loan and deposit portfolio. Like any successful business, commercial bankers have to grow their client base, provide outstanding customer service, and deliver profitable returns to their shareholders.

2. THE LOAN APPLICATION PROCESS

KEY ISSUES

Before you commence an application for a new or increased commercial loan, a simple acronym, **WARS** describes the essential components.

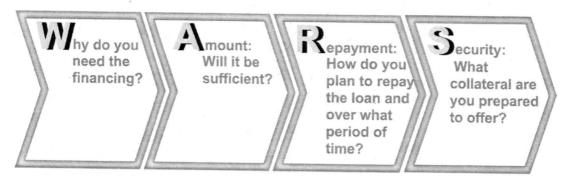

A short written presentation should be completed that outlines the financing requirement along with supporting company financial statements and/or projections and a current personal financial statement. Even if personal guarantees are not required, the depth of pockets of company principals will often be a key component of the bank's risk assessment process.

SPECIFIC GUIDELINES

Operating Line – New or Increased Facility

- ➤ Define purpose: Financing receivables, working capital requirements, etc.
- ➤ Indicate dollar amount and demonstrate need with monthly cash flow projections.
- ➤ Margin conditions: 75% eligible receivables, 50% cost of inventory.
- ➤ Work in progress (WIP) margin may be feasible.
- ➤ Provide receivable/payable listings along with inventory breakdowns.
- ➤ Interest rate (usually Prime + 1% or lower).
- ➤ Monthly loan administration fees (often negotiable).

Term Loan/Mortgage – New or Increased

- ➤ Indicate purpose and dollar amount required.
- ➤ Detail the repayment, term, and amortization desired. Amortization should match the economic life of the asset that is being financed.

➢ Cash flow coverage – should be a minimum of 1.25x.

➢ Property and equipment appraisals. Should be current and from credible professionals.

➢ Provide insurance details along with an environmental assessment and indemnity.

➢ Interest rate (fixed or floating): How does the offered rate compare to the other lenders?

➢ Application fees (sometimes negotiable).

Collateral

➢ GSA (General Security Agreement).

➢ Section 427 Bank Act (for inventory financing).

➢ Collateral mortgage/assignment of rents (for commercial properties).

➢ Chattel mortgage (for equipment loans).

Other Collateral Issues

➢ Personal guarantees: They will often be required, especially if the company does not have a track record of revenue/earnings growth and a strong balance sheet.

The bank will usually need a second way out if mishaps or serious problems occur. The primary way out is the company's ongoing ability to generate sustainable cash flow, backed up by the assets (accounts receivable, inventory, property) that fuel the cash generation.

If this process becomes seriously impaired, then recourse to other avenues of repayment (personal assets and resources) becomes an important second line of defense to a lender.

➢ Subrogations: These are encountered when shareholder loans are postponed to the bank's security interest. In effect, these equity funds may not be withdrawn or reduced without bank approval. Subrogated shareholder loans are often included in equity calculations for leverage test covenants.

➢ Assignment of life and/or disability insurance: The bank will often request assignment of key-person life and/or disability insurance, especially if succession plans are not clearly defined.

Financial Test Covenants

> These are often included in bank term sheets and offers of credit. They can best be described as financial benchmarks that need to be met on an annual basis, evidenced by the client's (audited or review engagement) financial statements.

> > Some examples:
> > Working capital ratio – minimum 2:1.
> > Debt to equity ratio – maximum 1.5:1.
> > Debt service coverage – minimum 1.25x.

> Each test covenant will have the relevant financial ratio calculation clearly defined.

Monitoring Requirements

> Operating lines of credit will involve prompt provision of monthly accounts receivable, accounts payable, and inventory listings. These are often accompanied by interim monthly or quarterly in-house financial statements so that ongoing performance can be measured against the prior year and budget (forecast).

3. BANK RISK ASSESSMENT

Once a loan proposal has been presented to the commercial banker, the internal loan application commences. This is a complex process with internal negotiation often taking place between the front-line bankers and the bank's credit department. A key ingredient of a company's successful loan approval is the completion of a detailed risk assessment by the front-line bankers for the credit department review.

Company owners can greatly enhance this process by providing a comprehensive information package to their banker. It is important that company owners gain a greater understanding of this risk assessment process. It is their company going under the microscope!

A bank's risk assessment process can be segmented into the following key areas, each with a check-list of questions and issues to consider:

> Company strategy.

> Market potential.

- Infrastructure and operations.
- Financial performance.
- Management capability.

COMPANY STRATEGY

- Is the company's competitive strategy based on:
    - Cost/price leadership?
    - Differentiation of products or services?
    - Focus on distinctive market segments?
- Which of the following generic corporate strategies have been implemented?
    - Diversification
    - Integration (Vertical or Horizontal)
    - Licensing
    - Outsourcing
    - Joint ventures or corporate alliances
- What are the company's sustainable competitive advantages?
- What are the key success factors necessary to prosper in the particular industry segment?

MARKET POTENTIAL

- What is the market size? Is there an over reliance on a few large clients or is there a well spread, balanced clientele?
- Is there reliance on a single or a few distributors?
- How stable is market demand?
- Assess the market acceptance of the company's products or services.
- How vulnerable is the company to competition, especially from 'big box' operations?
- What are current selling terms? Cash required on delivery or receivable terms?
- Infrastructure and Operations

> Consider environmental controls and regulations (present and proposed).

> Review fixed assets: location, characteristics, condition and adequacy. Are the premises owned or leased? Is adequate insurance in place?

> If applicable, what is the length of the manufacturing cycle and how controllable are manufacturing costs?

> Assess the price stability and availability of raw materials and other inputs.

> Review inventory: Mix, location, characteristics, condition and the ability to liquidate?

> Assess the adequacy, stability and quality of labor. Is the workforce unionized or is there potential for union involvement?

FINANCIAL PERFORMANCE

> How reliable and current is financial information? Have year-end financial statements been prepared by an accredited accounting firm?

> Are there any 'off balance sheet' issues to consider? Is there a large appraisal surplus in company owned land and buildings?

> Assess working capital adequacy and cash driver performance. Measure liquidity by inventory turnover, accounts payable settlement, and accounts receivable collection ratios.

> What is the relationship between debt and equity? What are the historical trends?

> Is there adequate equity to support expanding sales? Look for symptoms of over-trading (insufficient working capital base to support rapidly growing sales). Is there adequate cash flow to finance growth?

> What is the trend for revenues (volume and mix)?

> Assess revenue and gross margin performance and trends. Review control of expenses and determine the extent of fixed overhead?

> Are there any foreign exchange risks (export or import)?

> How adequate is the company's financial planning and related controls? Are regular (monthly, quarterly) financial statements completed on an in-house basis contrasting prior year, current year and budget performance?

MANAGEMENT CAPABILITY

➤ Examine the stability of owner's control: Are share holdings held on an amicable basis or is there potential for conflict? Is there a buy – sell agreement (along with an appropriate shot-gun clause) in place between the two controlling entities?

➤ The shot-gun clause keeps each party 'honest' by allowing Shareholder B to counter the offer made by Shareholder A at the same price, thereby dissuading a 'low-ball' offer for the other party's shareholdings.

➤ Do the owners have the ability to inject funds from sources outside the company?

➤ Do the company owners have 'hands on skills' to manage daily operations?

➤ Are there any related company borrowing requirements? What is their reliance upon the borrower, or the borrower's reliance upon them? A corporate family tree is always helpful in describing more complex business structures.

➤ Are aggressive expansion plans being contemplated? Have such expansion plans been carefully conceived – are they in line with company working capital, equity base and earnings capacity?

➤ Continuity and succession: Is there a clearly defined chain of command along with identified personnel who can step into the shoes of existing management?

4. DUE DILIGENCE CONSIDERATIONS

After the bank risk assessment process has taken place, there is another important step to take. The banker will be expected to perform due diligence with regard to the client, especially if the transaction involves a new relationship.

Due diligence can be defined as an organized and rigorous verification of all major components of a business transaction.

From a banking standpoint, the following areas would be reviewed:

Management

> Shareholder structure – active or passive involvement? How well do we know the individual shareholders?

> Any significant family relationship issues – pending divorce, ill health etc?

> Key management bios and historical on-the-job performance?

> Have meetings been held with the senior management team?

Financial

> Recent or planned capital expenditures – can the relevant assets be viewed?

> Reputation of accounting firm and partner signing year-end statements?

> Quality of finance support staff and reporting systems?

> Any contingent (cross guarantees) or unfunded liabilities (pension contributions)?

Infrastructure

> Recent visit to premises/operations?

> Inventory inspection if appropriate?

Clients and Markets

> Knowledge of key customers and competitors?

> Reputation in the marketplace?

> Relationships with key suppliers?

Legal

> Past or pending litigation?

> Patent or copyright protection issues?

5. EXTRACTS FROM A TYPICAL BANK COMMITMENT LETTER

BORROWER:

Marston Control Devices Ltd.

FACILITY:

Operating Loan Facility in the amount of $150,000, subject to the terms and conditions as outlined below.

RATE:

Bank Prime Rate plus one percent per annum (Prime+1%) floating, accrued from day to day, calculated and payable monthly, in arrears, based on a calendar year.

Prime Rate: 'Prime Rate' means the floating annual rate of interest established from time to time by the bank as the reference rate it will use to determine rates of interest on Canadian dollar loans, to borrowers in Canada.

MARGIN CONDITIONS:

Availability of the operating credit is subject to a maximum of:

75% of the bank's valuation of assigned accounts receivable after deducting those 61 days or more past due, accounts in dispute, inter- company accounts, contra accounts and the value of any prior ranking claims.

Plus:

50% of the bank's valuation at cost, of assigned inventory which is free and clear, excluding work in process, consignment inventory or inventory subject to any prior charge or claim. The maximum margin value of inventory will be $50,000.

MARGIN REPORTING:

Within twenty-one (21) days after the last calendar day of each month the following information should be delivered to the bank:

➤ A client certified aged list of outstanding accounts receivable identifying accounts in dispute, inter company accounts, contra accounts and the value of any prior ranking claims.

➤ A certified valuation of inventory excluding any items held on a consignment basis, and identifying all inventory subject to prior charges or claims in favor of other creditors.

➤ An aged list of outstanding accounts payable.

GENERAL CONDITIONS:

➤ Monthly Company prepared Financial Statements (Balance Sheet and Income Statement) are to be provided within 30 days of month end.

➤ Annual Company prepared Financial Statements (Review Engagement) are to be provided within 120 days of fiscal year end.

➤ A signed personal financial statement of John Marston to be provided concurrently with annual financial statements.

SECURITY:

Prior to any funds being advanced to the borrower by the bank, the following security documents should be executed, registered and delivered in a form and content satisfactory to the Bank.

➤ Appropriate documentation evidencing corporate authority.

➤ Registered General Assignment of Book Debts.

➤ Assignment of Inventory via Section 427 of the Bank Act.

➤ Registered General Security Agreement providing the bank with a first charge over all assets.

➤ Assignment of All Perils Insurance for Equipment and Inventory, with first loss payable to the bank.

➤ An unlimited personal guarantee from John and Ann Marston.

➤ Subrogation via promissory note of shareholder loans $96,000.

FINANCIAL COVENANTS:

➤ Capital expenditures are not to exceed $200,000 in any fiscal year without prior bank written approval.

➤ Total debt to equity ratio will not exceed 2:1 at any time. Equity is defined as retained earnings, subrogated shareholder loans, and share capital.

➤ Working capital ratio minimum 1.25:1 is to be maintained.

EXPENSES:

The borrower will be responsible for the following:

➤ All legal and other professional fees for searching, preparing, execution and registration of all loan and security documentation.

➤ All other costs and out-of-pocket expenses incurred by the bank in connection with the establishment and administration of the facilities and the obtaining of applicable security.

Please signify your acceptance of these terms by signing and returning the attached copy of this commitment letter.

USEFUL WEB SITES

www.cba.ca	Canadian Bankers Association – useful sections on business financing sources
www.strategis.ca	Comprehensive sources of financing section
www.firstresearch.com	Industry profiles and ratios
www.rbcroyalbank.com	Royal Bank business solutions centre
www.vancitycapital.com	Sub debt lending solutions

NOTES

CHAPTER 12
SURVIVAL STRATEGIES

OVERVIEW

Studies indicate that four out of five start-up companies cease to exist after five years.

This chapter is written on the premise that the more you know about 'the dark side of the moon' the less chance there will be that your company will become another statistic.

The chapter is divided into the following sections:

1. Causes of business failures

2. External warning signals

3. Internal warning signals

4. Turnaround strategies and options

1. CAUSES OF BUSINESS FAILURES

The authors have observed many successful companies prosper and expand. We have also seen companies 'come off the rails', sometimes permanently. Business failures can often be attributed to the following causes:

MANAGERIAL OR KEY EMPLOYEE PROBLEMS

> Lack of 'hands-on' management allied with a lack of inclination to jump in and fix potentially costly operational problems.

➤ Shareholder disputes aggravated by an absence of buy/sell agreements and shotgun clauses.

➤ Attempting an industry 'consolidation' play without the financial and operational resources to digest an acquisition target.

➤ Complex management and information systems installed at great cost and leading to greater disruption and little tangible benefit.

➤ 'Sole operator' management with no succession plans.

➤ Weak management communications and poor professional support.

PRODUCT OR MARKET DIFFICULTIES

• Venturing into new (offshore) markets without sufficient market research.

• Big Box and cross-border retailer incursions (Home Depot, Costco etc.)

• Poorly conceived new or 'follow on' product launches.

FINANCIAL WEAKNESS

➤ Embarking on an ambitious expansion project with too much debt and not enough equity.

➤ Significant receivables with protracted payment terms that result in stifled cash flow.

➤ Business failure of a supplier who provided critical components or equipment for a new contract.

2. EXTERNAL WARNING SIGNALS

➤ Adverse legal, political and regulatory changes 'coming out of left field'.

➤ Cultural and social changes that dramatically alter consumer preferences or product awareness.

➤ Failure to anticipate accelerating pace of technological change.

➤ Weakening of general economic conditions evidenced by inflationary trends, budget deficits, higher government taxes or reduced onsumer spending.

- ➤ Unexpected interest rate 'spikes' allied with tightening bank credit availability and stricter lending guidelines.

- ➤ Industry issues

  - ◆ Intensified competition overcoming historic barriers to entry.
  - ◆ Emergence of substitute products.
  - ◆ Increasing supplier and buyer power.

3. INTERNAL WARNING SIGNALS

A. FINANCIAL

- ➤ Tightened Liquidity evidenced by:

  - ◆ Delays in collecting accounts receivable, along with increases in bad debt expense.
  - ◆ Difficulties in meeting accounts payable obligations.
  - ◆ Bank overdrafts and locked-in (hardcore) operating credits.
  - ◆ Lack of an understanding of bank margin conditions.
  - ◆ Inventory buildup out pacing sales growth.

- ➤ Under Capitalization:

  - ◆ Increasing reliance on debt (bank and supplier) to finance operating losses.
  - ◆ Weakened retained earnings due to historical operating losses that have become 'acceptable'
  - ◆ Inability to attract additional capital. Existing shareholders are 'tapped out' and do not have deep pockets

- ➤ Lack of Financial Information:

  - ◆ Delayed year-end Financial Statements.
  - ◆ Absence of current monthly or quarterly financial statements.
  - ◆ Poor or non-existent cash flow monitoring and analysis.
  - ◆ Weak financial information control systems that have failed to keep pace with the company's growth and increasingly complex operations.

➤ Declining revenues, gross profit margins and earnings.

➤ Over-trading trends where working capital resources are insufficient to fund aggressive revenue growth.

➤ Unexpected increases in fixed costs.

➤ Dealing with too many banks and long-term lenders.

B. Products and Markets

➤ Inadequate current market research and failure to 'listen to the market place'.

➤ High concentration of sales to one, or a small handful of customers.

➤ Increasing failure to meet product sales and market penetration targets.

➤ Timing difficulties in launching new products.

➤ Overly complex distribution and selling strategies.

➤ Lack of ongoing product and service innovation.

C. Management and Key Employees

➤ Lack of clear business vision and guidance from key professional advisors and board members.

➤ High turnover rates among key employees.

➤ Delayed presentation of management and financial reports.

➤ Overly complex corporate structure with numerous subsidiaries and involved inter-company transactions.

➤ Obsession with tax-avoidance strategies.

➤ Employees with more than one boss or supervisor (matrix organizational structure).

➤ Delegation without control or feedback.

➤ Senior management abuse of benefits and compensation plans.

➤ Personal problems (divorce, family succession issues and disputes).

➤ Fraudulent activities which could include the following:

➤ Unexplained inventory shrinkage.

➤ Negligent financial reporting.

➤ Diversion of funds.

4. TURNAROUND STRATEGIES AND OPTIONS

In general, a turnaround strategy can be implemented by adopting the following process (with appropriate time lines):

1. Developing a recovery plan (from one to three months).
2. Implementation (three to six months) and then, stabilization of the business and return to growth (six months to a year).

It is crucial to commence the turnaround strategy on an urgent basis and craft the recovery plan as quickly as possible. The remaining implementation and stabilization steps will take more time. Companies are not turned around overnight; however, time is still a key consideration.

Note: Before beginning the turnaround process, solvency and viability need to be considered.

SOLVENCY

In most cases, a company is said to be *insolvent* if it is unable to meet its obligations as they become due *and* the net realization value of its assets does not cover its liabilities.

The Altman Z-Score – in the early 60's, Edward Altman, using Multiple Discriminant Analysis combined a set of financial ratios to come up with the Altman Z-Score.

Statistical techniques are used to predict a company's probability of failure using eight (8) variables from a company's balance sheet and income statements.

The following five (5) ratios are then weighted to derive the Z-score:

- EBIT/Total Assets
- Net Sales /Total Assets
- Market Value of Equity / Total Liabilities
- Working Capital/Total Assets
- Retained Earnings /Total Assets[1]

To return the company to a *solvent* state, some form of urgent external capital injection will need to take place.

VIABILITY

A *viable* company is one that is able to carry on profitable operations now and into the medium term. If the company is not viable, it is not worth expending valuable resources in an attempt to save it.

In assessing the viability of a distressed business, some key questions must be considered:

> ➤ Is there a sufficient depth of market (awareness) for the company products or services?

> ➤ Is there an effective sales force in place to market the product or service?

> ➤ Are reasonable gross margins being obtained?

> ➤ Does the business model now make sense (remember the dot com era?)

If the company is neither solvent nor viable, formal liquidation and wind-down will take place through Receivership or Bankruptcy proceedings. This process is complex, expensive and beyond the intention and scope of this book.

If a company is *solvent* and appears reasonably *viable*, the following steps will have to take place:

A. DEVELOPING THE RECOVERY PLAN

A critical first step is to complete a detailed **stakeholder analysis** – who are the key players that you must consider and work with if you are to survive?

These will include creditors (bank, suppliers, tax authorities), customers, employees, shareholders and management.

A quick and effective process is to 'map' these stakeholders according to their relative interest (in the situation) and their relative power. The following areas will then need to evaluated:

FINANCIAL RESOURCES

> ➤ Perform a critical assessment of current cash resources – check for excessively high accounts receivable and inventories. Can they be collected or reduced to generate cash?

> ➤ Assess the potential for sale and leaseback of fixed assets. This can often be another source of cash generation.

MARKETING RESOURCES

- Analyze revenue and profitability trends by market segment.

- Assess the 80:20 rule – which 20% of your clients provide 80% revenues?

- Verify product 'acceptance' in the marketplace (quality and customer need issues) – how effective is after-sales service?

- Check gross profit margin performance by major product lines.

OPERATIONAL RESOURCES

- If the business is a manufacturing operation, establish the percentage of production capacity that is currently used.

- Check for obsolete production equipment.

- Identify any procurement problems.

HUMAN RESOURCES

- Assess employee turnover and wage/salary costs relative to industry standards.

- Question senior management about the cause of the present downturn and how they would resolve it. What capability and commitment do they have to turn the company around?

- Can the company's organizational structure be simplified?

This process is summarized in the diagram overleaf.

Stakeholder Analysis

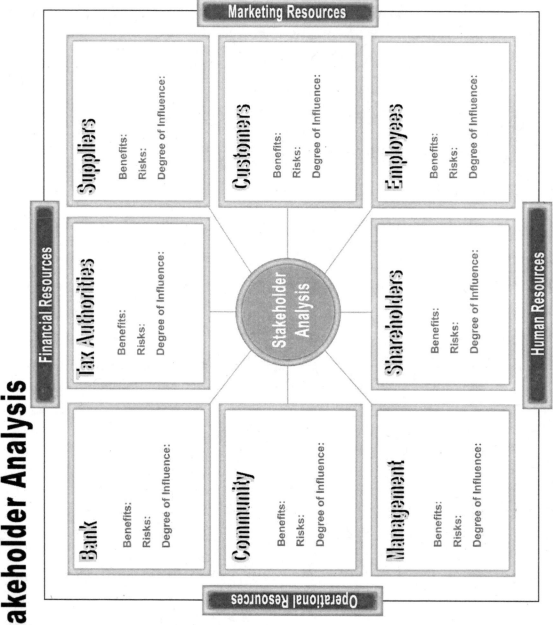

Marketing Resources

Financial Resources

Human Resources

Operational Resources

Suppliers
- Benefits:
- Risks:
- Degree of Influence:

Customers
- Benefits:
- Risks:
- Degree of Influence:

Employees
- Benefits:
- Risks:
- Degree of Influence:

Tax Authorities
- Benefits:
- Risks:
- Degree of Influence:

Stakeholder Analysis

Shareholders
- Benefits:
- Risks:
- Degree of Influence:

Bank
- Benefits:
- Risks:
- Degree of Influence:

Community
- Benefits:
- Risks:
- Degree of Influence:

Management
- Benefits:
- Risks:
- Degree of Influence:

B. IMPLEMENTATION AND STABILIZATION

Once the above stakeholder map and evaluation process has been completed, the following implementation steps, by functional area, can be considered:

FINANCIAL

- Increase revenues and market penetration through cost-effective advertising and lower prices.

- Reduce surplus and redundant assets by selective sell-off.

- Restructure debt by extending amortization, negotiating interest and/or principal holidays. In rare cases, debt forgiveness (usually with unsecured creditors) can be negotiated.

- Arrange equity injections through existing shareholders, possibly employees, outside investors, or government sources.

- Convince clients to provide up-front cash payments to pay for raw materials and supplies.

OPERATIONAL

- Restructure the company's organization to flatten reporting relationships and to re-align operations around a reduced number of product lines and/or market segments.

- Merge with or be acquired by a compatible company. Such a step can provide financial, operational and technical support to an ailing company.

- Initiate selective but effective cost-cutting measures. These could include pay concessions by employees (hopefully short-term pain for longer-term gain) or restructuring from salary to commission payment systems.

Useful Web Sites

www.ventureplan.com	Business survival strategies
www.smartbiz.com	Small business survival tips
www.ceoadvice.com	Implementing turnaround strategies
www.inc.com	Inc business magazine
www.entrepreneur.com	U.S business magazine – survival resources
www.profitguide.ca	Canadian business magazine – topical articles

Notes from text.

1. More information on the calculation can be obtained at www.creditguru.com/CalcAltZ.shtml

SECTION 4

STRATEGIC PLANNING

Business Diagnostics Overview

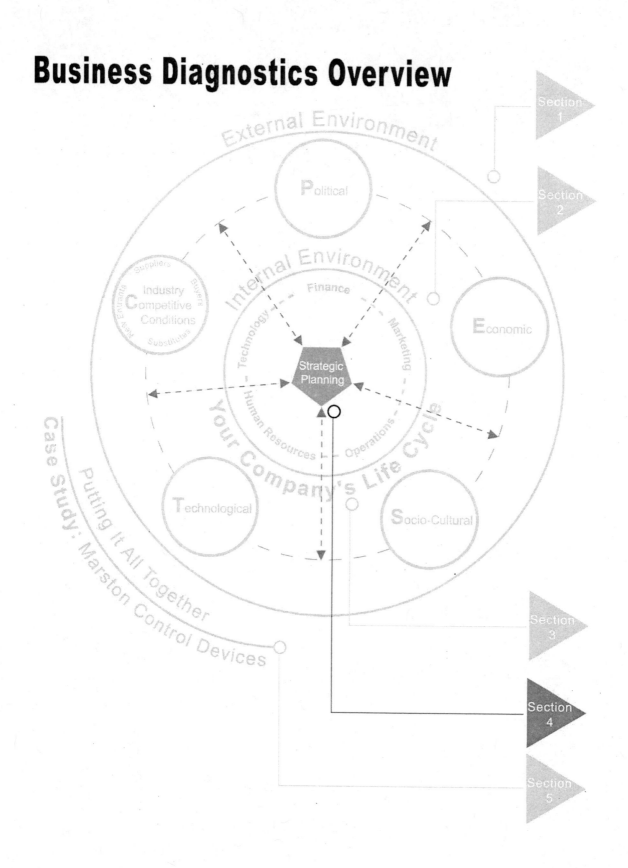

CHAPTER 13
THE BUSINESS PLANNING PROCESS

OVERVIEW

The business planning process is essential to the success of all enterprises. Some guidelines and tips in the crafting of effective business plans, with a strategic focus, are provided in this chapter.

While there are numerous templates and guides for business plan completion, developing a comprehensive plan is difficult due to the multitude of purposes such plans encounter.

To simplify (and demystify) the process, the following audiences have been segmented:

> **External** (Investors, Bankers, other Lenders)
>
> *and*
>
> **Internal** (Senior Management, Employees, Boards of Directors or Advisors)

Each audience will receive a different set of plans, which are detailed in the following sections:

External Audiences

```
┌─────────────────────────────┐
│  Enterprise Review Summary  │
└─────────────────────────────┘
              │
              ▼
┌─────────────────────────────┐
│   Strategic Business Plan   │
└─────────────────────────────┘
              │
              ▼
┌─────────────────────────────────┐
│ Offering Memorandum/Prospectus  │
└─────────────────────────────────┘
```

The Strategic Business Plan is common to both audiences, however **External Audiences** will typically receive an initial overview of an investment or banking opportunity by way of a short and simple 'Enterprise Review Summary' (ERS).

Following completion of the Strategic Business Plan and, if an investment opportunity is being pursued, a public offering and/or private placement process may be initiated via another set of documents, the Offering Memorandum and/or Prospectus.

Internal Audiences

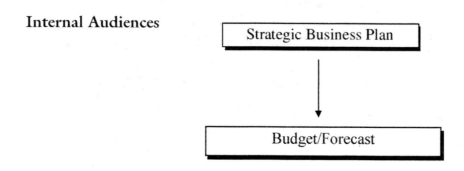

Internal Audiences will also have the opportunity to review the Strategic Business Plan, which acts as a foundation document. It is then accompanied by a detailed budget and forecast.

After reviewing the key features of these various planning documents, business plan features that either succeed or detract are examined.

Several tips on the effective packaging and presentation of plans are also presented.

1. EXTERNAL AUDIENCES

While clients and suppliers sometimes comprise the external audience, the focus on this presentation will be to *investors and/or lenders* because raising external funding remains a key challenge for many start-up and growing companies.

THE ENTERPRISE REVIEW SUMMARY (ERS)

The ERS concept is an expansion of the popular Business Opportunity Document (BOD) that has been championed by Denzil Doyle in his highly topical book "*Making Technology Happen*".

The ERS is a simple four – five page plain language document describing how an investor will make money from a product, service, or process generated by a company. If financing is required, the form of security and repayment will be described.

In essence, the ERS is an initial hook and is often fine tuned to form the executive summary in a formal Business Plan. The primary components of the ERS are:

- Overview
- Company description
- Current business and industry environment
- Products or Services (including any technology attributes)
- Markets (including segmentation, competitor evaluation and market tactics)
- Management
- Financial performance and projections
- Funding requirements
    - Investors – return on investment and exit point
    - Lenders – debt retirement and time frame

Each of these headings will be followed by a maximum of two to three paragraphs.

It is important to note that the pay-back section addressed to lenders would only be completed if the company was in a positive cash flow position.

Note: An example of an ERS is contained in Appendix C for the Marston Control Devices Ltd case.

THE STRATEGIC BUSINESS PLAN

In this section, the key components of a Strategic Business Plan are presented, along with some supplementary issues to consider within each section.

The structure can be summarized as follows:

- Executive Summary
- Description of the organization
- Management structure
- Products and Services
- Company external environment
- Industry analysis
- Company internal resources
- Competitor analysis
- Business strategy
- Financial feasibility and forecasts
- Market analysis
- Human Resources issues
- Operations & I.T assessment
- Appendices

EXECUTIVE SUMMARY

A one to three page overview of the complete strategic business plan. This section will include background, critical issues and key recommendations.

It is essential to have this section written *after* the other sections are completed.

An Enterprise Review Summary can be fine tuned to meet this requirement.

DESCRIPTION OF THE ORGANIZATION

Explains the type of company and provides a history if already in existence. It also describes the proposed form of organization including the company's mission, vision and objectives (if these have been articulated).

- Is the company's overall strategy consistent with prevailing industry opportunities and threats?
- Are the company's objectives consistent with its resources – financial, marketing, operations, technology, etc?

MANAGEMENT AND ORGANIZATIONAL STRUCTURE

This section will address shareholdings, executive, senior management and key employees. Information as to a board of directors or advisors will also be provided.

A brief stakeholder description and analysis can also be provided if required.

> Do senior managers have a shareholding interest in the company?

> Are the necessary marketing, operational, and financial skills in place or attainable in the near term?

PRODUCTS AND SERVICES

Existing products and services, along with potential 'follow on' offerings will be detailed here. An assessment of the company's present competitive advantage should be completed along with a summary of Intellectual Property (IP) strategies – if any.

COMPANY EXTERNAL ENVIRONMENT

This section will include a PEST analysis when external opportunities and threats are reviewed.

INDUSTRY ANALYSIS

The industry sector will be described along with current trends and market conditions. A brief 'Five Forces' analysis should also be provided here.

COMPANY INTERNAL RESOURCES

A brief 'Size-Up' should be completed with strengths and weaknesses detailed for the following functional areas:

> Finance

> Marketing

> Human resources

> Operations/I.T

> Research and development

COMPETITOR ANALYSIS

Primary and secondary competitors should be described along with an evaluation of their relative strengths and weaknesses.

BUSINESS STRATEGY

The organization's present strategic pathway should be described along with a review of alternative strategic directions that might be taken.

FINANCIAL FEASIBILITY AND FORECASTS

This section will involve a historical review of financial statements (for the last three to five years) including Balance Sheets, Income Statements, and Cash Flow Statements.

A ratio analysis should be completed with suitable commentary provided.

A forecast income statement (1 - 2 years) should be completed accompanied by a sensitivity analysis (best, expected, worst case). If possible, a forecast balance sheet should also be provided.

If this is a startup operation, a break-even analysis together with an indication of funding sources and allocation of proceeds should be completed.

SOME KEY QUESTIONS TO CONSIDER

- ➤ Does forecast EBT reveal steady growth in line with present industry norms?

- ➤ Will break even point be reached within two years if it is a start up operation?

- ➤ Is forecast ROI less than 20%? This would be considered weak from an investor's point of view.

- ➤ Does forecast EBITDA provide sufficient debt service coverage (from a lender's standpoint)?

- ➤ Will the projected balance sheets reveal too much leverage (high debt to equity ratio)?

MARKET ANALYSIS

This section details the company's customers and what type of competition will be encountered. Key features that should be included are:

- Identification of market segments.
- Analysis of target markets and profile of target customers.
- Methods to identify and attract customers.
- Selling approaches.
- Type of sales force and distribution channels.
- Tactics – the 6 P's.
    - Price, Product, Place, Promotion, People, Partners.

SOME ISSUES TO CONSIDER

- Is there a high dependence on a limited number of clients?
- Are there limited controls of pricing and distribution channels?
- Has a detailed competition assessment been completed?

HUMAN RESOURCES

This section will address current recruitment and training practices along with a review of compensation, performance management and incentive programs.

OPERATIONS AND IT ASSESSMENT

The operations segment will include a review of the business process, facilities and quality issues.

Risk management, and legal issues will also be addressed here.

IT issues will include e commerce requirements and computer technology applications.

SOME QUESTIONS TO CONSIDER

- ➤ Does the company have an appropriate location in relation to clients, suppliers, and employees, along with access to technology resources?

- ➤ Is there a dependence on a few key suppliers?

- ➤ Is there adequate capacity in relation to projected sales?

- ➤ Are there any potential environmental hazards?

OFFERING MEMORANDUM/PROSPECTUS

When companies decide to raise additional equity through, either an initial public offering (IPO), or private placement, various regulatory bodies will require the publication of an Offering Memorandum or Prospectus.

This documentation details the investment opportunity to potential investors together with a comprehensive disclosure of risk factors. Detailed capital and share structure information is also provided.

A more comprehensive review of the IPO and private placement process is not the intention of this book. Additional details can be obtained from local brokerage houses or venture capital firms.

2. INTERNAL AUDIENCES

STRATEGIC BUSINESS PLAN

We recommend the same format as established for external audiences but with more focus on the organization's strategic direction at the front of the plan.

The conventional approach is to spend time around strategic direction and vision – such a process would involve the following steps:

- ➤ Vision Statement – What we want to be.

- ➤ Mission Statement – What we do.

- ➤ Goals identification (i.e., revenue growth, customer satisfaction, technical excellence).

- ➤ Objectives – SMART (specific, measurable, achievable, realistic, time framed).

In our (somewhat unconventional) view, we feel that the whole Vision – Mission process is often just paid lip service, with no real enthusiasm to craft an appropriate strategic pathway.

Another solution is to engage the strategic planning participants with the following of three key questions:

> **What business are we really in?**

> **What is working well?**

> **What is our competitive advantage?**

We have found that this process leads to a high level of engagement among the planning participants.

At the back end of the plan, there should be two additional sections:

Key Action Items

These are applied to the various finance, marketing, operations/I.T, and human resources sections.

Implementation Steps

These are allocated to all the aforementioned categories indicating who will do what, when and how. The relative cost of these initiatives should also be determined.

BUDGET AND FORECAST

The **budget** is an internal document containing the balance sheet (quarterly), income statement and cash flow (monthly), together with capital expenditure forecasts and cost centre breakdowns by department.

The **forecast** is a monthly projection detailing key financial performance areas such as bookings, revenue, inventory, and cash flow.

In assessing the budget and forecast documents, two key steps need to be followed:

1) ESTABLISH SPECIFIC OBJECTIVES

Example:

> Increase revenues by 15% on an annual basis.

> Maintain gross profit margins at 45%.

These objectives will usually evolve from the key action items in the finance section.

2) SET UP TRACKING AND CONTROL SYSTEMS

Example:

> ➢ Quarterly review: Balance sheet, capital expenditures.

> ➢ Monthly review: Profit and loss statement, cash flow statement, etc.

SIX WAYS TO CREATE AN EFFECTIVE STRATEGIC BUSINESS PLAN

1. FOCUS ON THE MARKET

> ➢ Strive to be market driven (meeting customer needs) rather than promoting the product feature/service offering. The potential of the marketplace and resulting revenue/earnings is far more important.

> ➢ Demonstrate the users' benefit rather than promoting the product/service virtues and innovation. If the offering can provide significant cost savings to clients (e.g., a pay-back period under two years), this translates to a significant user benefit.

> ➢ Are you able to fix a customers 'pain' with the provision of your unique product or service?

> ➢ Determine the potential client's interest in your product or service. This interest can be demonstrated by letters of support or appreciation.

> ➢ New products or services can be offered as prototypes to potential users selling at or below cost in exchange for benefit feedback and endorsements.

> ➢ Document booking orders with supporting data indicating the number of customers who have committed to purchase. This allows you to provide a convincing projection of the "rate of acceptance" for the product or service and the pace at which it is likely to be sold.

2. ANTICIPATE INVESTORS' OR LENDERS' REQUIREMENTS

Investors

- ➤ Who are your potential investors? Are they friends and family, angels, venture capitalists or strategic corporate investors?

- ➤ Understand the investors' primary objectives. These can be summarized as follows:

    - ♦ Exit strategy (cashing out): Investors do not expect to receive a steady flow of dividends from small, fast-growing companies. Their return will be the profit gained from a successful exit either by selling their appreciated share holdings once the company goes public or by redeeming shareholdings once the company is sold.

    - ♦ The price and relative percentage ownership: The potential value of the company is usually based on projected earnings (EBIT) or cash flow (EBITDA) five years into the future, in conjunction with an appropriate earnings or cash flow multiple. The relative percentage shareholding derived will mirror the investor's required rate of return which, in turn, reflects the risk of the venture.

    Examples:

    A company with new products and unproven management: 40%+ annual returns are usually required.

    A company with developed products and proven management: 25% to 35% annual returns are usually required.

- ➤ Provide evidence of a strong proprietary position (i.e., patents, copyrights, trademarks in place).

- ➤ Detail the use and specific allocation of the investors' proceeds.

Lenders

Remember the **WARS** acronym (Chapter 11 – Financing):

- ➤ Why is financing required?

- ➤ Amount of funds required?

- ➤ Repayment: Over what timeline and from what source (ongoing earnings or sale of assets?)

- ➤ Security: What company assets are available?

Does the lender have a clearly defined 'alternate way out' and would this involve the provision of personal guarantees?

3. EMPHASIZE MANAGEMENT DEPTH AND CAPABILITY

Does your management team have:

- Proven industry experience?

- Previous start-up experience?

- No unexplained gaps in resumes?

- A track record in successfully bringing new products or services to market?

It is critical that the reader of the plan understands that the management team has been fully involved in the strategic business planning process. Business owners sometimes borrow heavily from sample business plans or delegate the complete task to outside consultants.

It is critical that the key elements of the plan be prepared by the company management team (not just the founder). External resources can be engaged to fine tune and complete the final plan documents.

4. CLEARLY DEFINE YOUR CUSTOMERS AND COMPETITORS

Customers

- Segmentation – Which are the most attractive segments?

- Targeting – Who is buying from you?

- Preferences – What do they buy from you?

- Timing – When do they buy?

- Criteria – Why do they buy?

Competition

- Demonstrate your knowledge of the competition and how you are keeping track of them (latest product offerings, price discounts, etc.) on an ongoing basis.

5. PREPARE REALISTIC FINANCIAL PROJECTIONS

- Investors and lenders will focus on the accuracy and integrity of your financial numbers.

➤ Projections and revenues, gross margins and earnings have to be carefully supported by assumptions that are reasonable and that can be defended.

➤ Complete 'best-expected-worst case' scenarios. You can be sure that your numbers will be stress tested by the investors or lenders.

➤ Ensure there is a correlation with industry norms and benchmarks

➤ Avoid 'spreadsheet overkill' with excessive analysis and scenarios creating a numerical 'smog' that deters and confuses the reader.

6. COMPLETE THE EXECUTIVE SUMMARY (LAST)

This is the most important section of your Business Plan. People will read it first and formulate their initial impressions based on these critical pages.

If you do not get the potential investor's attention with the Executive Summary, they will likely not read the rest of the business plan.

Your ERS (Enterprise Review Summary) can usually be fine tuned to meet the information requirements of the Executive Summary.

PACKAGING AND PRESENTATION TIPS

The Strategic Business Plan provides outsiders (investors, lenders) with a first impression of your company and its management team. The following tips will assist you in presenting a professional and effective package to your audience:

Appearance

➤ Professional binding and printing are important. Avoid a too lavish or glossy appearance, which might be misinterpreted (excessive spending? snow job?).

➤ The cover should bear the company's name, address, and date issued. Maintain strict copy numbers (maximum 20). This allows you to keep track of the number of copies circulated.

➤ Length – we suggest 25 to 30 pages maximum. Again, a carefully prepared Executive Summary (maximum two to three pages) is crucial in convincing the reader to proceed with the rest of the document.

➤ Background and supporting information can be included in an additional binder that would be available as part of the due diligence process.

Presentation

- Wherever possible, obtain an appointment with your prospective audience and get face to face when delivering the Business Plan. This strategy allows you to highlight the opportunity in person. Keep the meeting brief and leave the plan for the readers to review at their own leisure.

- Clearly identify the person who provided you with the opportunity to meet your audience (your lawyer, accountant, etc.)

- A more formal presentation, perhaps involving a panel of investors, could involve a brief PowerPoint presentation (maximum 20 slides), which summarizes the key elements of the plan (Refer to Chapter 9).

Note

- Slides should be in bullet form with short and concise sentences (maximum six per slide) in order to retain the audience's attention.

- Always rehearse this type of presentation.

- Set up presentation equipment early and test.

- Have back-up overhead slides and projector just in case 'Murphy's Law' strikes.

CONCLUDING COMMENTS

The strategic business planning process can be complex and will involve a number of stakeholders, notably the senior management team. It has to be realized that the end result will not be a Soviet style five-year plan, deeply engraved in stone.

Rather, it will be the creation of a broad roadmap that will assist the navigation of many twists and turns.

We leave you with a few thoughts from Henry Mintzberg who sets out the five 'Ps' of Strategy from his recent book *Strategy Bites Back*[1]

> ➤ Strategy is a *Plan* – a consciously intended course of action initiated by an organization.

> ➤ Strategy can be a *Ploy* – a maneuver to outwit the competition.

> ➤ Strategy is a *Pattern* – providing consistency of behavior.

> ➤ Strategy is a *Position* – to properly locate an organization in its operating environment.

> ➤ Strategy is *Perspective* – the way the organization views the world.

USEFUL WEB SITES

www.morebusiness.com	Business and Marketing plan templates
www.bplans.com	Comprehensive business planning tools including a PlanWizard that matches sample plans to your business

Notes from text.

1. *Strategy Bites Back* by Henry Mintzberg et al, FT Prentice Hall December 2004

NOTES

SECTION 5

CASE STUDY

Business Diagnostics Overview

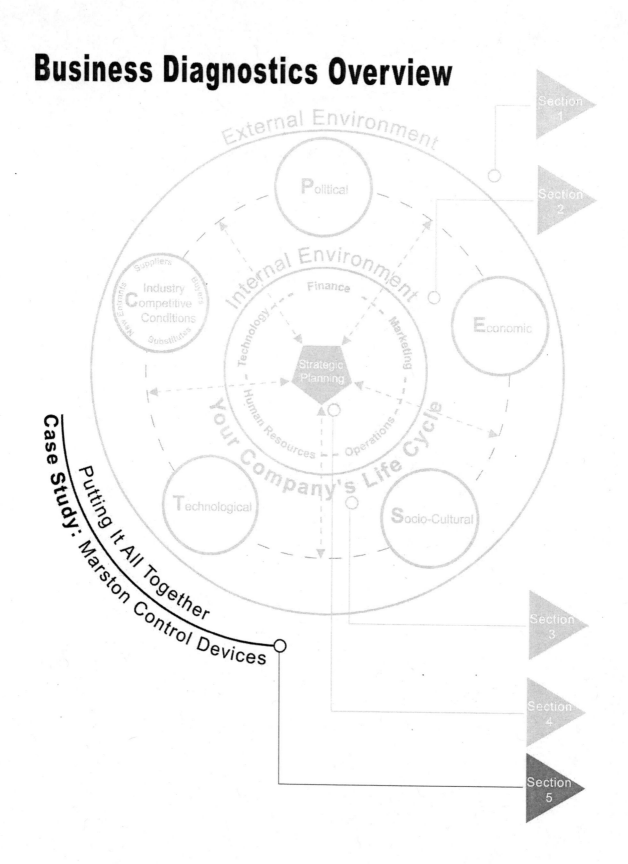

MARSTON CONTROL DEVICES LTD. CASE STUDY

OVERVIEW

In 1999, John Marston founded Marston Control Devices Ltd. (MCD) to design, manufacture, and market a specialized control component *(Sensorpro)* which was connected to industrial robots. The control component consists of a sealed unit housing sophisticated micro-controllers, which *send* control instructions to the robot and *receive* feedback on positioning, velocity and acceleration at the various robotic joints.

The *Sensorpro* units were sold to robot manufacturers for installation onto their industrial robots. The manufacturers, in turn, sold their product to large industrial automation systems companies who developed productivity manufacturing solutions for multi-national companies like Celestica and Nortel in Canada and Solectron, Flextronics and Honeywell in the USA.

COMMENTARY

Marston, a computer engineer by training, had graduated from the University of Southern California (USC) with a doctorate in Robotics. After academia, he completed various assignments, including a brief involvement with the team that successfully developed the Canadian space-arm used on the United States NASA space shuttle.

Upon relocating to Ontario for family reasons, he decided to put down some roots and formed his own manufacturing company to develop and market an innovative new robotic control component.

First year sales of $340,000 resulted in a net loss of $80,000; however, 2002 and 2003 showed substantial increases in both sales and net income.

Marston was an enigmatic individual, somewhat of a 'loner', and controlled his company with an 'iron hand'. He was involved in virtually every aspect of the business – design, production, sales, and finance.

He had left previous employers in California to start the firm because he had difficulty working as a team player, always wanting to be involved in the total project, not just a part of it. In the past four years, he had slowly begun to achieve his goals of financial gain and was slowly picking up business skills as the company expanded.

Marston and his wife together owned 100% of MCD. He recently made the following comments to a business associate:

> *I have been successful over the past few years primarily due to the high quality and unique design features of my product. As a result, Sensorpro commands a well-deserved premium price of 10 - 15% over the competition.*
>
> *Our units are currently priced at US $12,000 per unit which represents anywhere from 15% to 20% of the price of an industrial robot. Since there is a limited market here in Canada – most robots are imported – 90% of my market is in the United States.*

Competition was beginning to increase as United States robot manufacturers had adopted a 'backward integration' strategy and were developing their own control devices. A high profile example was Adept Technology, which had become a global leader in the manufacture, marketing and innovation of robots as well as control component products.[1]

Despite a downturn in economic activity in early 2002, the Japanese were now posing a threat, steadily moving into the United States domestic market.

> *One Japanese competitor firm recently obtained an order for 15 control devices on which we had bid. I was surprised at their lower price point but I still do not think they can match my unique design and performance.*
>
> *I have resolved not to get into price-cutting! This is a rapidly changing industry, and who knows what I will have to do in the future. There are only about eight firms — mine, three in Japan, three in the United States, and one in Europe, which produce similar control devices although the number of competitors may increase substantially over the next couple of years.*

Economic conditions in Fall 2004 were generally considered favorable – both the Canadian and USA economies were experiencing strong GDP growth; the only dark clouds on the horizon being the potential for a Federal Reserve interest rate hike due to concerns with the rapidly escalating US budget and trade deficits. The robotic control device industry was growing steadily as automation processes continued to be developed for a wide spectrum of applications, especially in the semiconductor and fiber optic manufacturing sectors.

> *While I have enjoyed reasonable relations with my component suppliers and there are many electronic supply houses from which to chose, they seem to have 'closed ranks'. Over the past few years, they have proven tough to negotiate with, which has been evidenced by a steady succession of component price increases.*

My steady sales growth over the past few years has resulted in a few 'loose ends' – our product catalogue needs updating, current quality control procedures need to be implemented, and we should establish a formal sales force structure. Past sales successes largely arose through my contacts in the industrial automation sector, electronics manufacturers trade shows and my USC alumni connections. Media interviews have been rejected to keep the competition at bay.

My production facilities are functional, although somewhat cramped. Our five-year lease comes due next month and I'm hoping my landlord is able to provide us with additional production space. The Sensorpro production process is quite streamlined (job shop assembly) and, over the past few years, I've invested in state-of-the-art assembly equipment. All orders are customized, so surplus component or finished product inventories shouldn't pose a problem.

My unique design and manufacturing techniques differentiate me from my competitors – I have not bothered with patent protection, preferring to maintain trade secrets and closely controlled software source codes. My product allows robot manufacturers to operate with more flexibility and more productivity than I ever anticipated. With continued 'pick and place' automation, notably in the chip manufacturing industry, the North American market should experience continued expansion. The demand is there and my product is at the forefront.

The production process requires reasonably skilled labor however; I have been able to condense the training process into 2-3 weeks. Most of my assembly workers have been casual, given the relatively short training horizon. Thankfully, there have been no union overtures to date. When I'm not available, my brother-in-law can adequately supervise both production and training. He is really the only one I can trust to ensure the operation is running smoothly when I'm not here. Of course, I never leave for more than a week at a time.

While MCD had experienced strong revenue and earnings growth over the past three years, Marston was experiencing continued cash flow tightness, evidence by bank overdrafts and occasional difficulty in meeting the payroll.

I am somewhat puzzled – my financial statements indicate that I run a profitable business with a reasonably strong Balance Sheet. Yet, I am always at the limit of my bank operating line and would be hard-pressed to declare any dividends to enhance my personal net worth and set aside funds for retirement.

Marston felt that he had come to the proverbial 'fork in the road' from a business expansion standpoint. He summarized his three strategic options as follows:

I can stay the course, producing the same product in the same marketplace, and work diligently to improve my profitability by ongoing expense reduction. My potential to improve gross profit margins appears low given the difficulty I continue to experience in negotiating material price reductions with my suppliers.

My other two options are as follows:

We can expand into Europe (where there is only one competitor) and license our technology to a strategic partner, ideally with close ties to European robotics manufacturers. We would stay with our existing product, but expand into a new market.

I understand that in 2004, major robot producers founded the European Robotics Association known as EUnited Robotics[2]. This association consists of robot manufacturers, system integrators and research institutes and plays a strong advocacy role with regard industry issues and R&D policy. They would be a useful starting point to seek out a potential licensing partner.

A further option would be to diversify our product line by developing a new control device product targeted at the medical devices industry. There is a new generation of robotic surgical devices (instruments, clamps and limb positioning tools) that could utilize a redefined Sensorpro technology platform. These devices are in various stages of FDA (Food and Drug Administration) approval.

This new generation of medical devices allows surgeons to view, cut, clamp, and suture from across the Operating Room sitting at consoles with joystick controllers that manipulate robotic arms above the operating table. Voice-activated robotic arms in the O/R are now being used, so the potential to develop new sensor technology in this emerging industry segment is huge.

Marston became even more enthused when he related some recent online research he had completed:

For example, the Da Vinci is a surgical robot enabling surgeons to perform complex surgeries in a minimally invasive way. It is FDA approved and used in over 300 hospitals in the Americas and Europe. The Da Vinci was used in at least 16,000 procedures in 2004 and sells for about $1.2 million[3].

University of Washington surgeon, Dr. Richard Satava, predicts that in the next 40-50 years surgery will be completely automated. The surgeon will manage an information system complete with robotics.[4]

Taking a deep breath, Marston summarized his future plans:

> *I feel that a combination of new market (Europe) and new products (control devices for medical robots) would be an aggressive, yet potentially rewarding move, especially as competition in our existing industry segment continues to intensify.*

> *I have developed a preliminary budget to launch such an expansion – initial cost estimates are in the $750,000 range, the main cost components being R&D to commercialize the medical robot control devices and marketing costs to expand into the European market. Raising these funds would have to involve outside investors as the various soft development costs would not qualify for bank financing.*

Marston recognized that he required strategic guidance and summarized his needs and concerns as follows:

> *First, I need to get a fix on my present corporate health, especially from a financial stand point.*

> *Then I need to attract some initial investor interest in my expansion opportunity – to do that, I need to prepare some form of brief summary document describing the investment opportunity and payback period.*

> *I also need to get a feel for what my company value is now and in the future (based on my expansion plans and resultant boost in earnings) and how much I would have to give up in terms of share ownership.*

THE NEXT STEPS

1. Based on the case and accompanying financial statements/ratio analysis, use the attached worksheets to complete an External and Internal size-up of MCD.

2. Using current financial statements, derive a current valuation for the company.

3. Prepare a four to five page Enterprise Review Summary (ERS) that summarizes the potential investment opportunity for the outside investor.

4. Based on the five-year, pro-forma income statements, complete a *preliminary estimate* of value and resultant ownership stake that an outside investor would acquire.

MARSTON CONTROL DEVICES LTD
Balance Sheet as of September 30, 2004
(thousands of dollars)

Assets	Sept. 2002		Sept. 2003		Sept. 2004	
Current Assets:						
Cash		$ 8				
Accounts receivable		76		170		392
Inventory		108		205		431
Prepaid expenses		9		14		17
Total Current Assets		201		389		840
Capital Assets						
Equipment, Furniture, Fixtures	224		258		273	
Less accumulated depreciation	(27)		(42)		(56)	
Net Capital assets		197		216		217
Other Assets						
Investment in Subsidiary		55		55		55
Total Assets		453		660		1,112

Liabilities & Owners' Equity	Sept. 2002		Sept. 2003		Sept. 2004	
Current Liabilities:						
Bank Loan Operating		$ 54		$112		$ 235
Accounts payable		24		47		276
Accrued salaries & wages		16		10		27
Income tax payable		8		21		14
Total Current Liabilities		102		190		552
Long-term debt						
Notes payable		240		240		240
Shareholder loans		27		47		79
Total Debt		369		477		871
Shareholder's Equity:						
Capital Stock		140		140		140
Retained Earnings		(56)		43		101
Total Owners' Equity		84		183		241
Total Liabilities & Shareholders' Equity		453		660		1,112

NOTES TO BALANCE SHEET

> Investment in Subsidiary relates to a $55,000 cash injection (2002) into Marston Voice Recognition Systems, a start up company that has yet to generate revenues or positive earnings.

> Bank operating credit is authorized at $150,000 secured by a General Security Agreement (GSA) and an unlimited guarantee from Mr. and Mrs. Marston. The facility is margined to 75% eligible accounts receivable and 50% inventory at cost to a maximum $50,000.

> Note Payable $240,000 relates to funds invested into the company by Marston's uncle, on a interest only basis at Prime + 4% with principal payments scheduled to commence in Fiscal 2005 repaid over a five year term ($48,000 annual payments).

> Shareholder loans increased by $32,000 in Fiscal 2004 through a cash injection from Marston's brother in law. The balance of shareholder loans were injected by Marston and his wife when the company was founded.

MARSTON CONTROL DEVICES LTD

Income Statement for the year ending September 30, 2004

(thousands of dollars)

	Sept. 2002		Sept. 2003		Sept. 2004	
Net Sales		$ 768		$ 1,554		$ 2,862
Cost of goods sold						
Opening Inventory	59		108		205	
Plus purchases	515		1,061		2,201	
Less closing inventory	108		205		431	
Total cost of goods sold		466		964		1,975
Gross Profit		302 39%		590 38%		887 31%
Operating Expenses:						
Salaries & wages		173		322		604
Rent		18		18		18
Utilities		14		17		23
Advertising		5		10		12
Travel		17		11		16
Insurance		6		7		8
Telephone		12		14		22
Bad debts		3		35		46
Inventory write down						38
Total operating expenses		248		$ 434		787
EBITDA		**54**		**156**		**100**
Depreciation expense		14		15		14
EBIT		40		141		86
Interest expense		16		18		20
Income before taxes (EBT)		**24**		**123**		**66**
Income tax expense		8		24		8
Net income		$ **16** 2%		$ **99** 6%		$ **58** 2%

NOTES TO INCOME STATEMENT

> Annual recurring capital expenditures are $20,000 per year.

> Property lease payments have been stable at $18,000 per year however, the lease renewal is pending with lease rates expected to increase.

MARSTON CONTROL DEVICES LTD
Statement of Cash Flow
For the year ending September 30, 2004
($ thousands)

Sept. 2004

Cash flow from Operations:

Net income	$58
Add:	
Depreciation expense	14
Change in accounts receivable	(222)
Change in inventory	(226)
Change in prepaid expenses	(3)
Change in accounts payable	229
Change in accrued expenses	17
Change in taxes payable	(7)
Net cash provided by Operations	**(140)**
Cash flows from investing activities:	
Purchase of capital assets	(15)
Change in other capital assets	
Net cash used by investments	**(15)**
Net Cash from financing activities:	
Proceeds from long-term debt	
Proceeds from shareholder loans	32
Net Cash from Financing activities	**32**
Net cash provided (used)	**(123)**

MARSTON CONTROL DEVICES LTD
Key Financial Ratios – $ thousands

	Sept. 2002	Sept. 2003	Sept. 2004
Profitability/Cash Flow			
Gross profit margin (Gross Profit ÷ Sales)	39.00%	38.00%	31.00%
Net profit margin (Net Profit ÷ Sales)	2.08%	6.37%	2.03%
Return on equity (Net Profit ÷ Equity)	19.05%	54.00%	24.07%
EBITDA – Capex	$34	$136	$80
Liquidity			
Current Ratio (Current Assets ÷ Current Liabilities)	1.97	2.05	1.52
Quick Ratio (Current Assets – Inventory) ÷ (Current Liabilities)	0.91	0.97	0.74
Stability			
Debt to Equity (Total Debt ÷ Total Equity)	4.39	2.61	3.61
Debt service coverage (EBITDA / Annual principal and interest pay-	3.4x	8.7x	5x
Total Debt / EBITDA	6.83	3.06	8.7
Efficiency			
A/R collection (Accounts Receivable ÷ Sales x 365)	36 days	40 days	50 days
Inventory turnover (COGS ÷ Inventory)	4.3x	4.7x	4.6x
A/P settlement (Accounts Payable ÷ Purchases x 365)	17 days	16 days	46 days
Growth			
Sales	119%	102%	84%
Net Profit		518%	-41%
Assets		46%	68%
Equity		118%	32%

MARSTON CONTROL DEVICES LTD

Projected Income Statement – 5 years

($ thousands)

	Sept.2005	Sept.2006	Sept. 2007	Sept. 2008	Sept. 2009
Sales	$ 3,500	$ 5,000	$ 8,000	$ 11,000	$ 15,000
GPM	32%	35%	36%	36%	36%
Gross profit	1,120	$ 1,750	$ 2,880	$ 3,960	$ 5,400
Operating expenses	1,290	$ 1,350	$ 2,160	$ 2,970	$ 4,050
EBIT	(170)	$ 400	$ 720	$ 990	$ 1,350
Net profit	(190)	$ 325	$ ·525	$ 740	$ 1,080

NOTES TO PROJECTED INCOME STATEMENT

➢ Marston's accountants have prepared detailed monthly Income statements for the first two years, followed by quarterly statements for the remaining three years.

➢ Detailed assumptions will have been documented to support the projections and would obviously be available for review by the investor.

➢ Highlight comments on the major Income statement items follow:

Sales:

The trend reflects the decision to expand into Europe (licensing revenues), the development of the new Medical control device platform and ongoing production into the existing Industrial Automation market. Detailed breakdowns by product line and geographic area are provided to the investor via separate schedules.

Gross Profit margin:

Improvement reflects impact of the higher margin Medical device product line – again, detailed assumptions on a product line basis would be provided to the investor.

Operating Expenses:

The larger % of operating expenses to sales in Fiscal 2005 reflects non-recurring tooling and initial market/product development costs associated with the proposed expansion. Detailed schedules with supporting assumptions are provided.

MARSTON CONTROL DEVICES LTD
Projected Balance Sheet
As of September 30, 2005 ($ thousands)

Assets	Sept. 2005
Current Assets:	
Cash	(45)
Accounts receivable	570
Inventory	400
Prepaid expenses	18
Total Current Assets	943
Long-term Assets	
Equipment, furniture fixtures	473
Less accumulated depreciation	(85)
Net fixed assets	388
Other Assets	
Investment in Subsidiary	100
Total Assets	1,431

Liabilities & Shareholder's Equity	
Current Liabilities:	
Accounts payable	356
Accrued salaries & wages	55
Income tax payable	
Total Current Liabilities	411
Long-term debt	
Notes payable	190
Shareholder loans	29
Total Debt	630
Shareholder's Equity:	
Capital Stock	890
Retained Earnings	(89)
Total Owners' Equity	$ 801
Total Liabilities & Shareholder's Equity	$ 1,431

NOTES TO PROJECTED BALANCE SHEET

Marston's planned allocation of the $750,000 new investment proceeds is summarized as follows:

- Additional Fixed Assets (new manufacturing equipment) – $200,000.

- Coverage of forecast Fiscal 2005 operating losses – $190,000.

- Partial repayment shareholder loans and Note payable – $100,000.

- Additional injection into subsidiary for voice recognition research – $50,000.

- Reduction in Bank operating credit – $ 200,000.

DUE DILIGENCE BY THE POTENTIAL INVESTOR

- While the Capital stock figure has increased by $750,000 (from $140,000 to $890,000), Marston's stated allocation of proceeds appears to be inconsistent.

- In the Enterprise Review Summary (ERS) the $750,000 proceeds are allocated towards R&D and the European market expansion costs.

While the new manufacturing equipment ($200,000) and Fiscal 2005 operating losses ($190,000) are reasonable "uses" of the investment proceeds, the investor has to ask if the other proposed allocations of investment proceeds are appropriate.

- Bank operating credit repayment – $200,000: is the bank applying pressure to have its exposure reduced by lowering the amount of *authorized* credit available to the company?

- Is it reasonable to have Marston and his family withdraw $100,000 from the company by way of reductions in Shareholder loans and Notes payable?

- Is it realistic for Marston to re direct a portion of the investor proceeds ($50,000) into the dormant subsidiary company?

THE BUSINESS ENVIRONMENT

	Opportunities	Threats
Political		
Economic		
Societal		
Technological		

INDUSTRY CONDITIONS

Competitive Conditions

	High	Neutral	Low
Threat of new entrants			
Bargaining power of customers			
Bargaining power of suppliers			
Threat of substitutes			
Intensity of competition			

Key success factors?

Blue Ocean potential?

Focus?

Divergence?

Compelling tagline?

FINANCIAL SIZE-UP

	Strengths	Weaknesses
Profitability and Cash Flow		
Liquidity		
Stability		
Efficiency		
Growth		

MARKETING SIZE-UP

	Strengths	Weaknesses
ANALYSIS Product/Services Review Market Segment Asssessment Unmet Customer neeeds?		
MARKET POSITIONING Competitor Evaluation Pricing considerations Product mix issues Placement (Distribution) Promotion requirements People needs Partnering opportunities?		

OPERATIONS SIZE-UP

	Strengths	Weaknesses
Operational capability *Process* management *Facilities* management *Inventory* management *Quality* management *Risk* management *Project* management		
Legal issues		
Use of technology		

HUMAN RESOURCES SIZE-UP

	Strengths	Weaknesses
Human Resource function Recruitment and Hiring Training and Development Compensation, Performance and Incentives		
Leadership issues Organizational Structure Skills Development Teams and Teamwork Management Capabilities Appreciative Inquiry potential Mentoring opportunities		

TECHNOLOGY SIZE-UP

	Strengths	Weaknesses
Technology concept and product		
Intellectual property issues		
Potential risk factors		
New Technology Assessment ?		

STRATEGY REVIEW (1)[5]

	Opportunities	Threats
Present Course (Status Quo) **Define:**		
Alternative Directions? 1) 2) 3)		
Best Option: **Rationale:**		

STRATEGY REVIEW (2)

Resources to achieve goals?	
Finance	
Marketing/Sales	
Human Resources	
Operations	
I.T	
Management	
Best Practices to adopt?	

STRATEGY REVIEW (3)

Key Action Items	
Finance	
Marketing	
Operations	
Human Resources	
Technology	
Innovation	
Other	
Implementation Steps	
Responsibility?	
Time frame?	

232 Business Diagnostics 2nd Edition

Notes from text.

1. http://www.adept.com/

2. http://www.eu-nited-robotics.net

3. http://en.wikipedia.org/wiki/Medical_robot#History

4. www.pbs.org Light Speed special report on remote surgery – 2004

5. We wish to acknowledge the CAMC (Canadian Association of Management Consultants) whose Comprehensive Exam strategic planning model has been referenced in the development of our Strategic Review process.

APPENDIX 1

EXTERNAL AND INTERNAL 'SIZE-UP'

MARSTON CONTROL DEVICES LTD.

THE BUSINESS ENVIRONMENT

	Opportunities	Threats
Political	◆ European Community open borders ◆ Potential for government R&D grants and/or export assistance? ◆ Continued internationalization of industry segments	◆ FDA regulations re new medical devices product line? ◆ Adverse European regulatory environment re new licensing arrangements?
Economic	◆ Stable economy, strong GDP growth	◆ Potential for interest rate hikes/economic downturn? ◆ Adverse exchange rate movements Canada vs. USA ? Canada vs. Europe?
Societal	◆ Increased investor awareness re growth potential in the Industrial Automation and Medical Device sectors ◆ Health-care industry experiencing cost containment issues with associated benefits to the medical devices industry segment.	
Technological	◆ Continued opportunities to enhance Sensorpro technology platform ◆ B2B enhancement of Buyer or Seller relationships (procurement efficiencies)	◆ Technological compatibility re European product end users ◆ Increasing pace of technological change, with need for increased R&D resources. ◆ Potential ability of clients to turn into competitors – backward integration

INDUSTRY CONDITIONS

Competitive Conditions

	High	Neutral	Low
Threat of new entrants ♦ Unique technology platform should deter potential new entrants ♦ High capital costs to set up manufacturing operation			X
Bargaining power of customers ♦ Robot system manufacturers have the ability to produce competing products (backward integration)	X		
Bargaining power of suppliers ♦ Supplier 'cartel' pricing arrangements and inability to switch to alternate sources of supply	X		
Threat of substitutes ♦ Clients are unlikely to switch to substitutes without incurring substantial costs			X
Intensity of competition ♦ Industry segments growing rapidly ♦ Larger competitors will have more financial and R&D muscle	X		

Key success factors

➢ High quality and proven reliability of the *Sensorpro* control device
➢ CEO's industry connections and reputation
➢ Unique technology protected via trade secrets

Blue Ocean potential?

➢ Given the competitive nature of the robotic control component industry sector, especially the industrial automation sub-sector, it would appear there is limited opportunity to apply the criteria of Focus, Divergence or Compelling tag-line

FINANCIAL SIZE-UP

	Strengths	Weaknesses
Profitability and Cash Flow	Positive profit (EBIT) and cash flow (EBITDA) performance over past three years Reasonable Return on Equity Modest annual capital expenditure requirements	Alarming drop in Gross Profit margin from 38% to 31%. Reason? Weakening EBIT/EBITDA performance over past year. Can the trend be reversed?
Liquidity	Positive Current ratio, although a declining trend has been observed over past fiscal year – 2.05 to 1.52. Industry average?	Softening Current and Quick ratios reflecting increased inventory levels. A/R composition and age? Inventory breakdown between raw materials, W.I.P and finished products?
Stability	Comfortable debt service coverage (5x) Shareholder loans have increased – future source of additional equity? Earnings fully invested – no dividends paid out If Notes payable and Shareholder loans are postponed, Debt:Equity ratio improves to 0.99:1	High (unfavorable) Total Debt: EBITDA ratio – 8.7 years to retire debt from present annual cash flow Investment in subsidiary – current financial statements available? Strength? Weakening Debt:Equity ratio increasing from 2.61 to 3.61:1
Efficiency	Lengthened A/P settlement – if agreed by suppliers, then OK – a source of cash	Lengthening A/R collection (36 to 50 days over past two years). Reason? While inventory turnover has been stable, inventory levels have doubled over the past year – allied with inventory write down expense, this is a significant 'red flashing light'
Growth	Significant Sales growth over past three years	Weakening earnings growth (-40%) Reason? Asset and Debt growth exceed growth in Equity

MARKETING SIZE-UP

	Strengths	Weaknesses
MARKET ANALYSIS **Product/Services Review** **Market Segment Assessment** **Unmet Customer needs?**	Appears to meet USA robot manufacturers need for flexibility and productivity	No formal review of product portfolio has taken place. A detailed segmentation analysis for existing and proposed new markets is required
MARKET POSITIONING **Competitor Evaluation** **Pricing considerations** **Product mix issues** **Placement (Distribution)** **Promotion requirements** **People needs** **Partnering opportunities?**	Potential access to new and diverse markets? Seen as a 'price leader' due to demonstrated quality Apparent high quality Reasonable delivery track record Direct delivery to robot manufacturers (no middle link to slow down the process) Sales successes through trade shows and industry contacts – relatively low cost	Increasing competition from Japan + potential client backward integration? Unlikely to maintain present premium price as competition intensifies Continued vulnerability to suppliers Absence of warranties Does not have knowledge of existing competitor product lines Outdated sales catalogue Previous media problems No formal sales force No Sales & Marketing management function. Potential licensee in E.U but no formal investigation done yet

OPERATIONS SIZE-UP

	Strengths	Weaknesses
Operational capability		
Process management	Streamlined, relatively simple production process (job shop) Relatively modern equipment Custom orders, no speculative production runs	Not ISO 9000 certified
Facilities management	Local labor force quality and reliability appears OK Reasonable access to U.S. markets	Questionable ability to expand Imminent lease expiry
Inventory management		Inventory writedowns
Quality management		Absence of formal Quality Assurance and Quality Control procedures. Unaware of Six Sigma process
Risk management		Key Person Insurance in place? Business Loan Insurance in place? Business Interruption Insurance in place?
Project management		No formal PM process in place
Legal issues	Corporation with limited liability and limited recourse to the shareholders	Potential minority shareholding for brother-in-law needs to be documented
Use of technology	Appears to use latest CAD/CAM processes	Manufacturing equipment obsolescence issues? Absence of proper MIS (Management Information Systems) No knowledge or apparent interest in B2B benefits re procurement and sales.

HUMAN RESOURCES SIZE-UP

	Strengths	Weaknesses
H-R function		
Recruitment and Hiring	Non unionized workforce	Potential for employee turnover (casual versus full time) and resultant 'commitment issues'
Training and Development		Lack of ongoing training and development programs
Compensation, Performance and Incentives	Relatively simple compensation programs – casual wages and hiring process	No profit-sharing plans or provision for key employee minority share options
		No enhanced compensation arrangements for brother-in-law (key support person)
Leadership issues		
Organizational Structure	Back-up management support from brother-in-law	Too flat an organizational structure – Marston is spread too thin
Skills Development	Strong client credibility (NASA background)	Questionable professional support – legal and accounting
Teams and Teamwork		Inflexible – 'iron hand'
		Management by crisis allied with weak Bank relationship
		Unable to delegate
Management Capabilities	'Hands on' style – knows all aspects of the business	
Appreciative Inquiry potential		Nominal – too much focus on crisis management
Mentoring opportunities		No Board of Directors or Advisors
		Lack of succession plan

TECHNOLOGY SIZE-UP

	Strengths	Weaknesses
Technology concept and product	Existing technology platform has unique design and cost features with a proven manufacturing track record Is developing a product migration strategy – Medical Control Devices that will have higher functionality and higher price	Needs a comprehensive technology development plan for the new Medical Control Device product line
Intellectual Property issues	Trade Secret strategy (non-disclosure) has minimized IP costs Proposed European licensing arrangements will allow Marston to test and exploit new market with the selected licensee unlikely to become a future competitor	No patent protection No IP plan Selection process of European licensee – criteria and due diligence? Time frame to put in place? Risk of competitors attempting to re-engineer product
Potential risk factors		Limited provision for R&D expenditures to date Potential emergence of a superior technology? Need to get a fix on duration of product life-cycles – existing and proposed new product lines Potential to lose key employees to competitors?
New Technology Assessment?		Very preliminary work started on the new medical device product – no real sense of the R&D requirements yet

STRATEGY REVIEW (1)

	Opportunities	Threats
Present Course (Status Quo) Manufacturer of control devices for the USA industrial automation sector	Potential for government R&D grants and/or export assistance? Internationalization of industry segments Additional enhancement of Sensorpro technology platform. Further leverage industry connections and reputation.	Increasing pace of technological change, with need for increased R&D resources. Potential ability of clients to turn into competitors – backward integration Technology protected by trade secrets but vulnerable to patent infringement suits?
Alternative Directions? **1)** Expand industrial automation into E.U via license agreement **2)** Diversify into Medical Devices sector with new product line **3)** Combine both E.U and Medical Device expansions	Expand into a new market with a proven product Increased investor awareness re growth potential in the Medical Device sector Enjoy the benefit of both product and market expansion revenue opportunities	At this stage, no research or due diligence has been completed with regard to a potential EU partner Technological compatibility re European product end users? FDA regulations re new medical devices product line? Considerable research and development required. Launching a too aggressive expansion without adequate financial, managerial and operational resources

Best Direction

'Stay the course' – but investigate the product and market expansion options via detailed market assessment studies.

Rationale

This appears to be the wisest course of action given the limited resources available to the company at this point in time.

MCD is a successful player in the industry automation sector with exciting expansion potential which has to be carefully researched. Increased financing or additional equity, on an incremental basis, could be attracted to fund the costs associated with the assessment of the new market and or product opportunities.

STRATEGY REVIEW (2)

Resources to achieve goals?	
Finance	Assess need for increased bank credit and external funding to launch future product/market expansions
Marketing/Sales	Consider need for an external consultant to complete Market Development plans
Human Resources	Assess the need for an outsourced CFO to tighten financial reporting and controls
Operations	Evaluate cost of new CAD system and office network
Management	Need to explore potential for new CEO appointment with JM and his receptivity in assuming role of CTO (to develop new medical device product line)?
Innovation	There will be an ongoing need to invest in R&D resources, especially if the medical devices option is explored.
Best Practices to adopt?	Investigate potential for local university grad students to work on the new Medical Device applied research. Investigate joining TEC to benefit from external mentoring Assess need for Six Sigma to enhance production quality and delivery process

STRATEGY REVIEW (3)

Key Action Items	
Finance	♦ Provide bank with Enterprise Review Summary to obtain additional financing and/or new equity to fund product/market expansion research and due diligence.
	♦ Provide A/R, A/P and Inventory listings along with Interim Financial Statements to bank in order to negotiate renewal and possible increase of operating line.
	♦ Analyze GPM (gross profit margin) performance and isolate factors causing decline.
	♦ Analyze inventory position – the negative decreasing turnover trend and higher year-end inventory levels are cause for concern, especially as orders are typically on a custom basis
Marketing	♦ Prepare a formal marketing plan which will include a segmentation of the three target markets:
	♦ Existing Industrial
	♦ New European Industrial
	♦ New Medical Devices
	♦ Complete assessment of competitors (existing and potential) in each segment.

STRATEGY REVIEW (3)

Key Action Items	
Operations	♦ Complete ISO 9000 certification and develop Quality assurance/control procedures. ♦ Negotiate and document formal minority shareholder agreement with brother-in-law. ♦ Arrange Key Person and Business Interruption insurance through insurance broker. ♦ Engage a seasoned commercial realtor to research prevailing lease rates and other available production space that would accommodate forecast growth. ♦ Negotiate lease renewal with expansion option or relocate.
Human resources	♦ Document succession plans with lawyer/accountant in conjunction with Key Person insurance. ♦ Establish a board of advisors with members selected for their ability to add value to the expansion plans and investment-raising initiatives. ♦ Consider adding senior finance and sales/marketing positions to the company once the investment round has been completed.
Technology	♦ Establish a technology development plan for the new medical devices control system (brother-in-law to complete). ♦ Have lawyer complete I.P plan and research cost and logistics of patent protection for the new product line. ♦ Investigate potential E.U licensee selection process through industry association contacts.
Implementation Steps?	♦ The priority, responsibility and timing to implement the above action items would be allocated between John Marston and James Lewis.

APPENDIX 2

CURRENT COMPANY VALUATION

MARSTON CONTROL DEVICES LTD.

CURRENT COMPANY VALUATION— MCD

Two approaches are appropriate based on the financial information provided:

ASSET VALUATION ($ THOUSANDS)

Modified Book Value approach – based on Fiscal 2004 Balance Sheet:

Total Assets less any Intangible Assets (Investment in subsidiary)

$1,112 - $55 = $1,057

less:

Total Debt (excluding shareholder loans)

$871 - $79   = $792

$1,057 - $792 =   **$265 Book value**

EARNINGS VALUATION ($ THOUSANDS)

Fiscal 2004 EBIT = $86 (Average for the three-year period = $ 89)

Cap rate 25% (4x multiple) – based on subjective review of 'value factors'

No apparent surplus assets (term deposits, etc.)

Estimated value $86 x 4   =   **$344 Earnings-based value**

Reconciliation: Asset approach $265

Earnings approach $344

ISSUES TO CONSIDER

> A market based valuation is not appropriate due to MCD's relative small size and absence of meaningful price/earnings multiples.

> A cash flow valuation would involve assumptions as to future annual cash flows and eventual company sale proceeds at some future date – these future cash flows would then be discounted back to a present value using an arbitrary discount rate. A number of these variables may be difficult to substantiate.

> The current company value appears to lie in the $325,000 + range. Marston and his accountant could argue that:

> the subsidiary investment does indeed have a tangible value (based on R&D completed to date)

and

> the cap rate at 25% is unduly conservative – a 20% rate (5x multiple) would yield an higher value ($430,000).

> If Marston was attempting to sell the company 'as is', the final result would be driven by negotiations between buyer and seller and their respective motivations.

> The adverse financial trends observed in our internal Size-Up would require detailed explanation to the potential investor. A compelling case would have to be made by Marston that the company does, indeed, have solid future prospects.

APPENDIX 3

ENTERPRISE REVIEW SUMMARY

MARSTON CONTROL DEVICES LTD

ENTERPRISE REVIEW SUMMARY—MCD

THE OPPORTUNITY

Marston Control Devices Ltd. (MCD) was founded by John Marston in 1999 to design, manufacture and market a specialized control component (*Sensorpro*) which is installed on a wide variety of industrial robots.

Over the past five years, MCD has achieved significant sales growth, notably in the USA robot component marketplace. The company has built a strong reputation for product quality and durability at the same time, maintaining a price leadership position despite increasing foreign competition.

Having achieved an established niche in the industrial automation arena, MCD is now embarking on an aggressive diversification strategy. A European licensing partner is being identified to take the *Sensorpro* product line into the European robot component market. At the same time, a new control device product is being developed for the robotics controls sector within the medical devices industry.

The company owners (John and Ann Marston) are seeking a capital injection of $750,000 from outside investors to assist with the company's expansion and diversification strategy.

TECHNOLOGY

The technology platform was developed by John Marston after a successful assignment as project manager for the *Canadarm* NASA project.

The *Sensorpro* units are assembled via a job shop process utilizing state-of-the-art CAD/CAM production techniques. The product's unique design and manufacturing techniques have eliminated the need for expensive patent protection, especially as software source codes are closely controlled.

Recent research and development has led to the development of a new medical robotics control component which is now at the engineering prototype stage. Pilot production runs and user evaluations are scheduled within the next six months prior to formal product launch into the medical devices industry.

PRODUCTS

The original *Sensorpro* control device has undergone various refinements over the past three years (improved durability and functionality) and has received strong buyer acceptance in the industrial automation marketplace. Recognizing increasing competitive pressure from offshore manufacturers, a carefully researched product migration strategy has been formulated – the development of a new control component targeted at the Medical Devices industry. A new generation of robotics surgical devices (instruments, clamps and limb positioning tools) are being developed that will utilize a redefined *Sensorpro* technology platform.

Development of this new control component will add improved functionality to the robotics arms that allow surgeons to view, cut, clamp and suture using remote joy stick controllers away from the operating table.

Internet-initiated and voice-activated robotics arms in the operating room are now on the radar screen with huge growth potential associated with these emerging technologies.

MARKETS

The first generation of *Sensorpro* units have been successfully sold to robot manufacturers for installation onto their industrial robots. The manufacturers, in turn, sell their product to large industrial automation systems companies who develop productivity manufacturing solutions for multi-national companies like Celestica (Canada) and Solectron and Flextronics (USA).

There are only eight firms —MCD, three in Japan, three in the United States, and one in Europe which produce similar control devices although the number of competitors is expected to increase in the near term.

Significant sales growth has occurred in the USA as the industrial automation sector continues to develop a wide spectrum of applications, especially in the semiconductor and fiber optic market segments.

While the North American industrial automation market is expected to grow, intensifying competition has led to our decision to expand into two new markets:

> ➤ Existing *Sensorpro* product – expansion into the European market is now appropriate, given limited competition. A strategic partner is being identified who will be provided with a license to produce the *Sensorpro* technology platform and then target selected European robotics manufacturers.

> ➤ A new control component for the medical devices industry is being developed and targeted at the new generation of medical robotics systems that are used in hospital operating rooms.

Initial customer evaluation will take place in Ontario, Canada followed by market development across North America.

E-Commerce sales and procurement opportunities will be exploited via affiliation with a major B2B service provider.

MANAGEMENT

Company operations are closely supervised by John Marston and his brother-in-law, James Lewis. Both have degrees in Computer Engineering. Marston has 20+ years in the robotics industry, gaining international recognition and prestige through his successful project management career in NASA.

Marston is actively involved in every aspect of the business, including new research and development initiatives along with supervision of daily operations.

MCD is 100% owned by Marston and his wife, however consideration is being given to selling a small minority interest to James Lewis.

INVESTMENT AND PAYBACK

The $750,000 investment proceeds will be utilized to expedite the R&D associated with the medical control component together with marketing costs relating to the European expansion program. The proceeds are required by December 31, 2004.

The investor can either take equity through a share-issue, or secure proceeds via a convertible debenture.

Projected Income Statements – 5 years*
(thousands of dollars)

	Sept. 2005	Sept. 2006	Sept. 2007	Sept. 2008	Sept. 2009
Sales	$ 3,500	$ 5,000	$ 8,000	$ 11,000	$ 15,000
GPM	32%	35%	36%	36%	36%
Gross profit	$ 1,120	$ 1,750	$ 2,880	$ 3,960	$ 5,400
Operating expenses	$ 1,290	$ 1,350	$ 2,160	$ 2,970	$ 4,050
EBIT	-$ 170	$ 400	$ 720	$ 990	$ 1,350
Net profit	-$ 190	$ 325	$ 525	$ 740	$ 1,080

* Detailed revenue and expense projections are available for review by the investor as part of their due diligence process.

EXIT STRATEGY

Given the forecast growth in revenues and earnings in the next five years, there will be attractive exit opportunities, either through an IPO, or a combination of dividends and share buy back. Annualized ROI in the 25-30% range is anticipated.

APPENDIX 4

PRELIMINARY ESTIMATE OF
FUTURE VALUE FROM
AN INVESTOR'S PERSPECTIVE

MARSTON CONTROL DEVICES LTD.

PRELIMINARY ESTIMATE OF FUTURE VALUE FROM AN INVESTOR'S PERSPECTIVE – MCD

The following approach is suggested based upon the Projected Five year Income statements ($ thousands) that were provided in the case.

Year Five EBIT   = $1,350

Industry earnings multiple assumed   5 x

Assume investor's desired ROI = 30% compounded annually over 5 years

Calculations

MCD Future value in Year Five $1,350 x 5   = $6,750

Future value investor's cash injection

$750   @ 30% over 5 years*   = $2,785

*($750 x (1+ 30)5

Equity interest $2,785
                            ———   =   41%
                            $6,750

ISSUES TO CONSIDER

> Given all the assumptions, one could be forgiven for asking 'is this voodoo science'?

> Negotiations would likely take place in the 45% (minority interest) to 55% (majority interest) range.

> Voting share allocations have to be considered as the investor would want significant voting rights.

> The investor's $750,000 cash injection could be set up on a 'quasi debt' basis via a convertible debenture. This is a debt instrument that allows the holder to appoint a Receiver in the event of default and, also, convert the debenture to shares (common or preferred) at some pre-determined date.

> While this 'equity stake' calculation is 'back of the envelope' in its relative lack of complexity, it does provide a basis for opening negotiations that would eventually be supported by more formal valuation engagements completed by professionals.

REFERENCES AND RECOMMENDED READINGS

Where material has been referenced and/or adapted, the necessary written permissions have been obtained from the respective publishers.

Denzil Doyle *Making Technology Happen* 5th edition Doyletech Corporation

Longenecker, Moore, Petty and Donlevy *Small Business Management – An Entrepreneurial Emphasis* I.T.P. Nelson Thomson Canada Limited 1998

Beamish and Woodcock *Strategic Management* 5th ed. McGraw Hill Ryerson Limited 1998

Industry Canada, Strategis website *Steps To Growth Capital* 1999

ISBN 1552127b4-8

9 781552 127643